SpringerBriefs in Statistics

For further volumes:
http://www.springer.com/series/8921

Mike Allerhand

A Tiny Handbook of R

 Springer

Mike Allerhand
Department of Psychology
Centre for Cognitive Ageing and Cognitive Epidemiology
George Square 7
Edinburgh EH8 9JZ
UK
e-mail: michael.allerhand@ed.ac.uk

ISSN 2191-544X   e-ISSN 2191-5458

ISBN 978-3-642-17979-2   e-ISBN 978-3-642-17980-8

DOI 10.1007/978-3-642-17980-8

Springer Heidelberg Dordrecht London New York

Cover design: eStudio Calamar, Berlin/Figueres

Printed on acid-free paper

Springer is part of Springer Science+Business Media (www.springer.com)

Acknowledgment

The work was undertaken by The University of Edinburgh Centre for Cognitive Ageing and Cognitive Epidemiology, http://www.ccace.ed.ac.uk/, part of the cross council Lifelong Health and Wellbeing Initiative (G0700704/84698). Funding from the United Kingdom Biotechnology and Biological Sciences Research Council (BBSRC), Engineering and Physical Sciences Research Council (EP-SRC), Economic and Social Research Council (ESRC) and Medical Research Council (MRC) is gratefully acknowledged.

Contents

Chapter 1
Introduction to R

Abstract Introduction to R and programming concepts.

Keywords Functions · Arguments · Libraries · Packages

1.1 Why Command Lines and Scripts?

R has a command-line interface, not a point-and-click GUI (graphical user interface).[1] A GUI is easier to learn, and is the best way to interact with graphics. But you can be more expressive with command lines. The commands have a syntax. It's a language, and like any language the more fluent you are the more expressive you can be. Ultimately it gives you a wider range of possibilities than a GUI.

At some stage you will have to write a program or "script", several lines of commands. This seems laborious at first but becomes rewarding as you develop scripts you can re-use. It is quite possible for example for an R script to read data, fit some models, generate some tables and graphics, and even typeset the results. Then you can reproduce the whole process with a single keypress. You can regenerate the whole paper with different data. You can send your work to a colleague so they can see your results and replay the process by which you obtained them.

The best way to learn R is to use it. It is not something you can easily learn by reading about it. But it helps if you have a roadmap, which is the aim of this tiny handbook. Run the commands in R. Experiment with them.

---

[1] There are GUI front-ends for R, such as package Rcmdr, but to get the full benefit of R learn to use the command line.

M. Allerhand, *A Tiny Handbook of R*, SpringerBriefs in Statistics,
DOI: 10.1007/978-3-642-17980-8_1, © Springer-Verlag Berlin Heidelberg 2011

1.1.1 The R Console

When you start R you see a GUI, a window with a few icons and menus at the top. Those are just for setting up preferences like the size of the text. The main part of the window is the R "console", which is the command-line interface. All data manipulation and statistics is done using commands entered at the console.

Using R as a Calculator

Start R[2] and type in some arithmetic expressions hitting the Enter key after each. The point of this is to get a feel for the way R interprets commands. For example:

> 3 * (2 + 2)

[1] 12

> 3ˆ2 + 3

[1] 12

   R interprets each line as soon as you hit the Enter key and immediately displays the results.[3] R uses conventional arithmetic expression syntax. If in doubt use brackets to enforce operator precedence.[4]
   After you have entered several commands like this, try the up/down arrow keys. These scroll up and down your command history. Notice you can scroll up to a previous command, change it in some way, and run it again by hitting the Enter key. Try editing a previous command using the left/right arrow keys and the backspace and delete keys. Other useful shortcuts are the key combinations: Ctrl+a (go to start of line), Ctrl+e (go to end of line), Ctrl+u (clear the current line), Ctrl+l (clear the console window), and the usual Windows copy and paste combinations: Ctrl+c and Ctrl+v.

---

[2] On a Windows PC you'll find it in the All Programs menu. Using Linux you can just type R. If necessary install it from http://www.r-project.org/. The base installation requires about 35 Mb of disk space. Versions are provided for all platforms.

[3] If a line is not syntactically complete when you hit Enter R will display the continuation prompt '+' and wait for you. The number in square brackets is called the counter, and numbers the first item on each line of output as a convenience for when there are many items over several lines.

[4] For example 3ˆ2 + 3 versus 3ˆ(2 + 3).

1.1.2 Variables

You can temporarily store values in variables. It is the same idea as a variable in algebra, say x, where x can stand for any number. In R you create a variable simply by assigning[5] a value to a name[6]

> *x = 3*

Think of this as "the value of x becomes 3". If you had already created a variable named x, whatever value it had before is now lost; its value now is 3. That value is used when you use x. For example:

> *y = x + 1*

Here a new variable named y is created, and its value becomes whatever value x has plus 1. The value of x is unchanged by this.

The current value of a variable is displayed when you type its name at the console:

> *x*

[1] 3

> *y*

[1] 4

1.1.3 Functions

Functions process data. Functions were invented to modularize processing. They encapsulate frequently used subroutines of instructions, giving them a name so

---

[5] We will use the assignment operator =, but note that R provides other assignment operators <- and ->. The <- operator was used for S at Bell Labs because the terminal they had happened to have a key corresponding to the ASCII underscore that printed as a back arrow, (http://www.developer.r-project.org/equalAssign.html). It has remained in use by S and R traditionalists, and appears in most published R code. The = operator was introduced in 2001 for compatibility with S-Plus, C, Java, and other languages. It's main advantage is one less keypress. It's main disadvantage is that R also uses it for function arguments passed as name=value pairs. The function calls: foo(x<-1) and foo(x=1) have slightly different effects: both pass the given value to the variable x within the function, but foo(x<-1) also assigns the value to x outside the function, where foo(x=1) does not.

[6] It is helpful to give computer variables meaningful names. In R the names of variables can include numbers as well as letters, but must not begin with a number. Names can also include dot as in: my.variable, and underscore as in: my_variable. (See: help(make.names)). Names are case-sensitive, so a variable named: my.variable is not the same as a variable named my.Variable.

they can be referred to and re-used within the program. The function is written once, but may be "called" (run) many times, each time with different "arguments" (input). Nearly everything that happens in R occurs through a function call.

You call a function by typing its name following by brackets containing arguments. For example the R function named sqrt, which operates on its argument to calculate and return the square root, is called like this:

> sqrt(2)

[1] 1.414214

Some functions take just a single argument, but many functions take several arguments separated by commas. The arguments can broadly be divided into two kinds: arguments that are used to supply data as input to the function, and arguments that are used to program the function and control its behaviour in some way.

When finished the function "returns" an object, a data structure containing the result of the operation. It may be helpful to think that there is just one way into a function, and that is via its arguments, and just one way out, and that is via the object that it returns. This object will be lost unless your program makes immediate use of it, either saving it by assigning it to a variable or by passing it as an argument to a function for further processing.[7]

When you call a function think of the program as temporarily jumping to wherever the function itself is stored, running the commands within it, and then jumping back to resume the program. Think of the object returned by the function as being substituted directly in place at the point where the function is called. For example in the following the objects returned by the respective function calls are used directly in the arithmetic expression just as if you had typed: x = 2+3.

> y = 4
> x = sqrt(y) + sqrt(y + 5)
> x

[1] 5

If you call the function without arranging to assign the value it returns to a variable, it appears on the command line as if you had typed it. Instead of assigning it, a common idiom is to pass a function as an argument to another function. Then the value returned by one function immediately becomes the argument that is input to another function. For example:

> x = −2
> sqrt(abs(x))

[1] 1.414214

---

[7] The last value is assigned internally to a variable named .Last.value.

Here there are two function calls. It helps to read this from the inside-out. First x is passed to a function named `abs` which calculates and returns the absolute value of its argument. That value then becomes the argument to `sqrt`.[8]

Functions are insulated in the sense that calculations within a function do not effect any values outside the function. For example `sqrt(y)` has no effect on the value of y. If you want to operate on y so it becomes its square root, you must explicitly assign the returned value to y, as in:

```
> y = sqrt(y)
```

1.2 Finding Functions and Getting Help

1.2.1 Libraries

R provides a great many functions, and you can also write your own. Functions and datasets are organised into libraries.

```
> library()      # List the libraries installed on your computer
> sessionInfo()  # List the libraries loaded into memory
```

Not all the libraries you have installed are loaded into memory when you start R. The point is to make R start up reasonably quickly with a core of the most useful functions. It is necessary to load a library into memory to makes its functions and datasets directly available for use within R.

```
> library("foreign")        # Load the library named "foreign"
> library(help="foreign")   # List the functions provided in "foreign"
```

1.2.2 Packages

The base installation includes the most commonly used libraries. Many more are available as packages for download. These extend R's functionality in many directions. It is best not to install the large amount of contributed packages straight away. Once you have the base installation and a reasonable internet connection it is easy to install packages[9] when you need them.

```
> install.packages("lme4")   # Download and install package "lme4"
```

---

[8] Passing a negative number, `sqrt(-2)`, causes a warning message because the result is NaN (standing for "Not a Number").

[9] See also function `install.views` in package `ctv`. By default packages are installed to C:\Program Files\R\R-*.*.*\library. If you do not have rights to install to that folder, use the `lib.loc` argument of `install.packages` and `library` functions to specify another folder.

1.2.3 Finding Functions

How to find the right function for the job and make it work properly? To find a function for, say, robust regression use your favourite search engine to find "r-project robust regression". It is likely to return links to R-help pages with the answer.

Some useful web sites	
http://www.r-project.org	R web site
http://www.cran.r-project.org	Downloads
http://www.rseek.org	Function finder
http://www.cran.r-project.org/web/views	Packages organised by task
http://www.tolstoy.newcastle.edu.au/R/	R mailing lists archive

If you know or can guess part of the function's name you can search the available function names for a partial match.[10] The apropos function searches for names amongst loaded functions. The help.search function searches documentation amongst all installed packages.

```
> apropos("^read")       # Search for function names starting with "read"
> apropos("\\.test$")    # Search for function names ending with ".test"
> help.search("read")    # Search the documentation for "read"
```

1.2.4 Getting Help

Once you have found the right function for the job you need to know what arguments it takes, what kinds of values you can pass to them, and what kind of object the function returns. Every function is documented and has a help page that can be displayed using the function help[11]:

```
> help.start()    # Manuals and reference guides
> help(t.test)    # Display the help page for function 't.test'
> ?t.test         # ...shorthand for the same thing
```

---

[10] Functions for searching generally take arguments that can include "regular expression" patterns. These include special characters such as ^ and $ which anchor character patterns respectively to the start and end of a string. See: help(regex). The character . also has a special meaning in regular expressions, and to match a literal . it's necessary to "escape" its interpretation using \\.

[11] See: help(help).

The help page for a function generally has sections called "Usage" and "Arguments" describing the arguments, "Details" describing the processing that the function carries out, and "Value" describing the object returned by the function. There is often a "See Also" section that contains links to the help pages of related functions. The "Examples" section at the foot of the help page illustrates aspects of the function that are not obvious from the preceeding material.

The help page is often terse and may at first seem almost cryptic. However the format is consistent and with practice can be read quickly. The aim is to provide just enough documentation to describe the function unambiguously without using too many words.

Usage

The "Usage" is a summary of the names and default values of the function's arguments. The "Arguments" section describes in more detail the kind of data that can be passed to each argument. Arguments can broadly be divided into two kinds: those that are used to supply data as input to the function, and those that are used to program the function and control its behaviour in some way.

Arguments that input data to the function are mandatory, meaning you must provide a value otherwise the function will display an error message. Many functions allow different kinds of input by providing alternative arguments. The usage section of the function's help page amounts to a synopsis of the ways a function can be called.

For example the usage for help(t.test) shows two S3 methods[12] with different arguments. These are two kinds of interface to the t.test function. One takes data passed as two vectors, x, y. The other takes data passed as a single vector and grouping factor in a "formula".

```
> ## Default S3 method :
> t.test(x, y = NULL, ...)
> ## S3 method for class 'formula':
> t.test(formula, data, ...)
```

Other arguments are used to control the behaviour of the function. This enables functions to accomodate special cases around their core generic functionality. For example the single t.test function can accomodate one and two sample t-tests, paired and un-paired t-tests, one-sided and two-sided hypotheses, and so forth.

---

[12] A "method" is object-oriented terminology for a function that is specialized for particular arguments. The "S3" refers to version 3 of the "S" language, upon which R is based. See: help(Methods).

The arguments that control behaviour are generally optional. You can omit optional arguments and accept the default values provided by the program. Or you can supply an argument to override the default.

The usage section of the function's help page indicates which arguments are mandatory and which are optional. The optional arguments are those given in the form: name=value. The "value" is the default that will be used for this argument if you choose not to provide a value. The default shown in the usage indicates the type of value that can be passed to the argument, (and further information about this is given in the argument section below).

Some arguments are shown with defaults that are numerical values. This indicates for example that you can override the default confidence level of 0.95 used in t.test by passing a different number to the conf.level argument:

> t.test(x, y, conf.level=0.99)

Some arguments have default values that are either TRUE or FALSE. Arguments like this are essentially switches that are turned on and off respectively by passing a "logical" value: TRUE or FALSE. For example the paired t test behaviour can be switched on by calling the function:

> t.test(x, y, paired=TRUE)

Some arguments take one of a prescribed set of options. For example the alternative argument may take either of the three options that are given as a character vector: c("two.sided", "less", "greater"). The first of these is the default option. This indicates that you can override the default two-sided alternative hypothesis by passing one of the other available options to the alternative argument:

> t.test(x, y, alternative="less")

Some arguments are shown with a default value of NULL. This indicates that the argument will not be used unless a value is supplied. In this case there is no clue in the usage as to what type of value the argument could take, but such information will normally be given in the arguments and details sections below. For example in t.test the arguments section indicates that y can take a numeric vector of data values. If no value is given y is not used, and the function carries out a 1-sample t test on the sample given as the x argument. Otherwise the function carries out a 2-sample t test on the samples given as the x and y arguments.

Argument names can be abbreviated when this is unambiguous, for example: alt="less". Arguments are passed to the function as a comma-separated list, and can be passed in any position within the list provided it is clear which argument is which. Consequently optional arguments can be passed in any order because they always have names. Mandatory arguments can be passed as values without names, but in that case must be passed in their correct positional order relative to any other mandatory arguments in the argument list.

Functions generally appear within arithmetic expressions, or as arguments to other functions, or simply as the right side of an assignment. But some functions have a special usage in which they appear on the left side of an assignment. Functions like this are indicated in the usage section of their help page as follows, for example for the names function:

> $names(x)$

> $names(x) <- value$

The first is the more conventional usage to "get" the names of x. The second indicates that this function can appear on the left side of an assignment, where its behaviour is to "set" the given value as the names of x. Functions with this kind of usage can typically be used either to get or set values in a data structure.

Value

The "Value" section describes the object returned by the function. Functions return a single object. Many functions return multiple values encapsulated within a list. Each component of the list has a name associated with it. For such functions the "Value" section of the function's help page describes the components and their names.

Unless the returned object is used in some way, either by assigning it to a variable or passing it directly as an argument to another function, it will display its value on the screen and then be lost.

1.3 R Projects

It is useful to keep each project in a separate folder. R can save your "workspace image" to that folder, all your current objects and command history, (up to the last 512 lines you entered). The next time you start R this can be restored exactly at the point where you left off, creating a running session. You can also email your R session to a colleague who can replay it.

1.3.1 Saving Your Session

When you quit R it offers to save your workspace image.[13] The objects are saved to a file named .RData, and the command history to a file named .Rhistory. These files are saved in the current "working directory", a folder that R will read and write to by default. It is important to set the working directory to your current

---

[13] You can also save your session using menu options: File > Save Workspace... and File > Save History... , or programmatically using the save.image and savehistory functions.

project folder. This is done automatically if you restart a previously save session. But if you start R from the Programs menu it does not know which folder you wish to use. Functions getwd and setwd are provided to get and set the working directory, but the easiest way to set it is using the menu: File > Change dir... If you wish to save your session be sure to set the working directory to a folder to which you have write permission.

Quit R with the function:

> q()

You should see a message: Save workspace image?. If you click No R quits without saving anything. If you click Yes R saves your session.

Restart R by double-clicking the .RData file in a project folder.[14] The session is restored as you left it, with your current working directory set to the project folder.[15]

1.3.2 Scripts

As an alternative to saving your workspace image, you may prefer to save the R commands for your analysis project as a "script". A script is a plain text file containing R commands. It can easily be re-run either by copying commands from the script file and pasting them into the R console, or by running the script as a whole using the source function. (See the options for managing scripts under the File menu).

As you develop scripts of commands you should add comments to them to remind you what the script is doing and what your original intention was. A "comment" is some explanatory text in a script that is not part of the program but helps make its meaning easier to read. In R a comment is any text on a line to the right of a # sign. The # and the comment are ignored by R.

---

[14] Your operating system may hide filenames that begin with a dot. On Windows use the menu item Tools > Folder Options... in any folder, and on the View tab ensure the option "Show hidden files and folders" is selected. On Linux list your files using ls -la.

[15] Commands you might want to run at startup can be stored in a file named .Rprofile in your project folder. For example commands to load certain libraries. See: help(Startup).

Chapter 2
Data Structures

Abstract Programming with R objects and data structures.

Keywords Objects · Data · Indexing · Data manipulation · Missing values

2.1 Data Structures

Data structures store your data, and functions process it. You might think of functions as actions and data structures as the objects acted upon. You might think of functions as operators on data structures. A function's input arguments, and the object it returns, are data structures.

A data structure is the programmer's interface to data organised in computer memory. R provides several kinds of data structure each designed to optimise some aspect of storage, access, or processing. The five main data structures are called: vectors, matrices, arrays, data frames, and lists.

2.1.1 Vectors, Matrices, and Arrays

Vectors, matrices, and arrays are all based on a contiguous sequence of cells. They are designed to enable fast access to a particular layout of data. A vector[1] is an ordered row of cells. A matrix is a rectangular two-dimensional layout of cells like a grid. An array is a layout of cells that allows more than two dimensions.

---

[1] A vector is the simplest data structure in R. Scalar values are treated as single-cell vectors. A vector can be thought of either as a row or column since under matrix multiplication in R it is interpreted in whichever way makes it conformable with the other argument.

M. Allerhand, *A Tiny Handbook of R*, SpringerBriefs in Statistics,
DOI: 10.1007/978-3-642-17980-8_2, © Springer-Verlag Berlin Heidelberg 2011

Each cell contains an item of data. The three main types of data[2] in R are called: "numeric", "character", and "logical".

Numeric data includes integers and decimal numbers.[3] Character data consists of strings[4] of keyboard characters. Logical data consists of "truth values"[5] denoted TRUE and FALSE.

The cells of a vector, matrix, or array must contain the same type of data. For example a numeric vector must contain numeric data, a character vector must contain character data, and a logical vector must contain logical data. If you try to combine data of different types within the same vector, matrix, or array it will automatically be "coerced"[6] to one data type.

Numeric vectors are generally used to store continuous data, often as the columns of a data frame. Character vectors are generally used to store names and labels. Factors (see below) are generally used to store categorical data and grouping indicators. Logical vectors are generally used during programming temporarily to store the results of applying some condition to data, which can then be used programmatically, (see the section on Indexing below).

2.1.2 Data Frames and Lists

Data frames and lists are collections of data structures linked together. They are designed as general-purpose containers for data.

---

[2] R also provides a "complex" type for complex numbers, and a "raw" type for bits. Cells with missing values may contain the special value "Not Available" (NA).

[3] Sometimes decimal numbers may be printed in exponential form, such as: 1.5e-08. This notation is used to print very small or very large numbers. The number 1.5e-08 is "1.5 times 10 to the -8", in other words 1.5/100000000.

[4] A string is a sequence of one or more keyboard characters, including spaces, and control characters such as \n (newline) and \t (tab), enclosed within quote marks, (double- or single-quotes). See help(backquote) for the list of control characters and further information about quote marks. Each cell of a character vector contains a string. For example: "apple", "apple", "orange".

[5] Logical values are types of data returned by conditional expressions such as 3 > 2, (TRUE as 3 is greater than 2), and "apple" > "orange", (FALSE as "a" is alphabetically less than "o"). TRUE and FALSE can be abbreviated to T and F. Note: don't make variables with these names as they will mask the abbreviations.

[6] The rules for type coercion are as follows: logical => numeric => character. For example mixtures of numeric and character data are forced to character data, in which case all numbers become quoted strings, such as: "3.14". The one exception to this is the special value NA (Not Available) used to signify a missing value. Functions with names that begin "is." are provided to test the type, and functions with names that begin "as." can be used to coerce the type. See apropos("^is\\.") and apropos("^as\\.").
as.numeric: Number strings => numbers. Non-number strings =>NA. TRUE=>1, FALSE=>0.
as.character: Numbers => number strings. TRUE=>"TRUE", FALSE=>"FALSE".
as.logical: 0=>FALSE, all non-zero numbers =>TRUE. Character strings =>NA.

A data frame is a rectangular layout of cells organised by columns. It is a collection of columns, all the same length, but which may be different types of vector. A data frame is most often used to store columns of raw data, some of which may be numbers, and some character data. Typically, but not necessarily, the columns are variables (and the column names are the names of the variables), and the rows are cases or observations. There is no particular requirement for one row per subject or case. Some columns may hold scores or names, others may be grouping factors used to indicate subjects, blocks, conditions or treatments, waves of repeated measures, and so forth.

A list is a collection of objects. The components of a list can be different types of data structure and can be of different lengths. A list is often used to pass a structured argument to a function and to return a multi-valued object from a function.

2.1.3 Creating Data

Data structures are created by reading data from some external source such as a file, database, or website. You can also create data within R for simulation and to create patterned vectors for use as a programming tool. This idea of "programming with data" occurs throughout R. For example a vector passed as an argument to a graph plotting function may be used to control the colours or shapes of individual points on a graph.

Creating Vectors

The simplest ways to create a vector are by combining, sequencing, or repeating vectors. The combine function c takes multiple vectors as arguments and combines them into one vector:

```
> x1 = c(2, 6, −1, 3.14, 0)            # Combine 5 single-cell numeric vectors
> x2 = c("apple", "apple", "orange")   # Combine 3 single-cell character vectors
> x3 = c(x1, x2)                       # Combine 2 vectors
```

The sequence operator : makes a numeric vector that is a sequence in integer[7] steps between its arguments. For example:

```
> x4 = 1:5
> x5 = 5:− 5
```

---

[7] See the seq function for making a sequence in fractional steps.

The repeat function `rep` makes a vector by repeating its argument, optionally as a whole or by repeating each cell. For example:

```
> rep(x4, times=3)   # Repeat as a whole
> rep(x4, each=3)     # Repeat each cell
```

Creating Matrices and Arrays

The simplest way to turn a vector into a matrix or an array is to use the functions `matrix` and `array`. For example:

```
> x1 = 1:16                                      # Vector
> x2 = matrix(x1, nrow=4, ncol=4)               # 4×4 matrix
> x3 = matrix(x1, nrow=4, ncol=4, byrow=TRUE)   # 4×4 matrix by rows
> x4 = array(x1, dim=c(4, 2, 2))                # 4×2×2 array
> x5 = array(x1, dim=c(2, 2, 2, 2))             # 2×2×2×2 array
```

Alternatively bind vectors together as the rows or columns of a matrix using functions `rbind` and `cbind`:

```
> x1 = 1:3
> x2 = c("apple", "apple", "orange")
> x3 = rbind(x1, x2)
> x4 = cbind(x1, x2)
```

Matrices and arrays are vectors with an attribute[8] named `dim` that describes the dimensionality of the layout of cells. The `dim` is a numeric vector that stores the number of number of rows and columns of a matrix, or the dimensions of each "margin" of an array. There is also a function named `dim` that is used to get or set this attribute:

```
> dim(x3)   # Dimensions (number of rows and number of columns)
> dim(x4)
```

---

[8] An "attribute" is a named piece of additional information attached to a data structure. Some attributes are part of the language in the sense that R functions understand them, notably `names` (named elements or columns) and `dim` (dimensions of matrices and data frames). Functions called `names` and `dim` are provided to get and set these attributes. However an attribute can also be any information you like, such as a comment or note attached to a data structure. Function `attr` is provided to get or set any individual attribute, and function `attributes` to get or set an object's list of attributes. Function `as.numeric` has the side effect of removing attributes. Function `c` also removes attributes except for `names`.

Creating Data Frames and Lists

The simplest way to create a data frame (besides reading data from a file) is to use the `data.frame` function to add column vectors to the data frame. The simplest way to create a list is to use the `list` function to add objects to the list:

```
> x5 = data.frame(x1, x2)
> x6 = list(x1, x2, x4, x5)
```

R has a simple GUI editor for data frames:

```
> fix(x5)                    # Edit a data frame
> x7 = edit(data.frame())    # Create a new data frame
```

R provides many data sets[9] as data frames.

A data frame can have column and row names. These are stored in attributes called `names` and `row.names` respectively.[10] For example the provided dataset named `swiss`:

```
> swiss              # The data frame
> help(swiss)        # Its help page
> dim(swiss)         # The dimensions (rows, columns)
> nrow(swiss)        # Number of rows
> ncol(swiss)        # Number of columns
> names(swiss)       # The column names
> rownames(swiss)    # The row names
> summary(swiss)     # A summary of each column
```

Creating Character Data

Some useful character vectors are provided for convenience[11]:

```
> letters    # Lower-case alphabet
> LETTERS    # Upper-case alphabet
```

---

[9] Most R packages provide some data sets as well as functions. Use function `data()` to see the data sets that are loaded by default. Data sets have help pages. For example the page describing the structure and variables of the data set named `swiss` is displayed by `help(swiss)`.

[10] The row names are just row numbers by default, but the attribute may be assigned a character vector of names using function `rownames`. Use `names` or `colnames` to get or set the columns names.

[11] See also: `month.name` and `month.abb` for the full and abbreviated names of the months; `date`, `Sys.Date`, and `Sys.time` for date and time strings.

Creating and formatting numeric strings:

```
> x = c(3.1, 0.05, 99)
> as.character(x)
> format(x)
> format(x, width=8)
> format(x, width=8, nsmall=3)   # Aligning the decimal point
```

Formatting character vectors:

```
> x = c("Apple", "Orange")
> toupper(x)                         # Convert to upper-case
> tolower(x)                         # Convert to lower-case
> format(x)                          # Left justify (default)
> format(x, width=8)                 # Field width
> format(x, width=8, justify="right")  # Right justify
```

Pasting strings together[12]:

```
> paste("x", 3.14, sep="=")              # Paste strings with a given separator
> paste(c("x","y"), c(3.14, 99), sep="=")  # Paste vectors element-wise
> paste("Item", 1:20, sep="")            # No separator
```

Searching and replacing strings[13]:

```
> grep("^J", month.name, value=TRUE)   # Match strings beginning with "J"
> sub("^J", "j", month.name)           # Replace "J" at start of string with "j"
```

Printing strings:

```
> x = c(3.14, 0, NA, 99)
> cat("Some numbers:", x, "\n")    # Concatenate and print
> print(x)                         # The default print method
> print(x, na.print=" ")           # Print missing values (NA) as blanks
```

2.1.4 Sampling Data

The sample function draws a random sample[14] of the cells of a vector, and returns the sample as a vector. The size of the sample is specified by the size argument.

---

[12] See function: strsplit for splitting strings into vectors.

[13] String pattern matching uses regular expressions. See: help(regex). See function substr for extracting and replacing characters at a given position within the string.

[14] A different sample is drawn each time a sampling function is called because the seed of the internal random number generator is updated automatically. If you want to draw the same sample you can set the seed. See help(set.seed).

Without this the default sample is the same size as the argument, so the default behaviour is to make a vector by permuting or shuffling the argument. For example:

```
> sample(1:10)
> sample(c("a", "b", "c", "d", "e"))
> sample(1:100, size=50)          # Random sample (n=50) from 1:100
> sample(100, size=50)            # ... the same thing (allowed for convenience)
> sample(0:1, size=50, replace=T) # Sampling with replacement
```

R provides functions to draw a random sample from several distribution families. For example the `rnorm` function draws a random sample from a normal[15] distribution. Its first argument specifies the sample size, and there are optional arguments `mean` and `sd` to specify the mean and standard deviation of the distribution to be sampled. The default parameters are `mean=0` and `sd=1`. For example:

```
> rnorm(50)                # Random sample (n=50) from N(0, 1)
> rnorm(50, mean=10, sd=2) # Random sample (n=50) from N(10, 4)
```

A careful reading of `help(rnorm)` suggests that `mean` and `sd` take vector values. When the meaning of this is not immediately clear it is often best simply to try it and see. For example:

```
> rnorm(4, mean=c(1, 100))   # Sampling from N(1, 1) and N(100, 1)
```

The vector passed to the `mean` argument is "recycled" (repeated) until its length matches the requested sample size, and then used to specify the mean of the distribution from which each observation is drawn. This idea of vector-valued arguments controlling individual observations is used in several places in R. (For example is to control the appearance of individual plotted points in graphics). A single valued argument is recycled so each observation in the sample is drawn from a distribution with the same mean. A multiple valued argument enables sampling from a normal mixture.

2.1.5 Reading Data

R provides several functions[16] for reading data from an external source such as a file, database, or website, and returning it as a single object. For example the `read.table` function is a general-purpose tool for reading tables of data from a plain text file,[17] and returning the data in a data frame.

---

[15] Equivalent functions for other distribution families include: `rt`, `rf`, `rbinom`, `rpois`, `rchisq`, `rexp`, `rweibull`, `rgeom`, `rhyper`, `rlogis`, `rbeta`, `rgamma`.

[16] See: `read.table`, `readLines`, `scan`, and related functions.

[17] Functions are provided in the `foreign` library to read data in several proprietary formats, including SAS, Stata, and SPSS. It is also possible to read data from certain databases such as MySQL. See the R Data Import/Export link from the HTML documentation displayed by `help.start()`.

These functions have a mandatory `file` argument to specify the data source. This may be a filename that is expected to be in the current working folder,[18] or may be a URL for data downloaded from a web site. Under Windows the `file` argument can be a call to the function `file.choose` which pops-up a Windows file locator, or may be the special value `"clipboard"` to paste data from the Windows clipboard.[19] For example:

```
> read.table("clipboard")                             # Paste from the clipboard
> read.table("http://www.some.web.site/myfile.txt")   # Download over http
> read.table(file.choose())                           # File locator
> read.table("myfile.txt")                            # Read a file in the working folder
```

The `read.table` function has several optional arguments to specify the file format. The most useful are: `header` to specify whether the first line is a column header or data, and `sep` to specify the column separator. The default values[20] of these arguments specify no header, and columns separated by blanks (one or more spaces or tabs). If for example the text file contains column headings on the first line and has comma-separated columns the options should be as follows:

```
> read.table("myfile.txt", header=TRUE, sep=", ")
```

Blank lines and comment lines (with the comment sign # at the left) in the file are ignored by `read.table`. Columns of numbers become numeric vectors[21] in the data frame. Columns of character data are by default converted to factors[22] in the data frame.

---

[18] If R displays a message that there is `"No such file or directory"` the most likely explanation is that your working directory is not pointing to the folder that contains the file. Set your working directory, or provide an absolute pathname to the file. Pathnames should either use forward slashes as in `"C:/path/to/file"`, or double backslashes as in `"C:\\path\\to\\file"`.

[19] See: `help(connections)` and `help(clipboard)`.

[20] Several variants of `read.table` are provided with slightly different defaults. See `help(read.table)`.

[21] If a column of numbers is intended to be a grouping indicator then it is necessary explicitly to convert the column to a factor, for example using function `as.factor`.

[22] Set argument `stringsAsFactors=FALSE` to override the default behaviour and keep columns of character data as character vectors. Use command `options(stringsAsFactors=FALSE)` if you wish to set this default behaviour globally. If a column of numbers contains characters such as '.' to signify a missing value, then the whole column is taken to be characters and converted to a factor. Set argument `na.strings` to '.' to override this and recode all '.' as `NA`, (see the section on Missing Values).

2.2 Operations on Vectors and Matrices

2.2.1 Arithmetic Functions

Arithmetic functions take a data structure argument and return the data structure after applying an operation element-wise to each cell. For example:

```
> x = rnorm(10, mean=5, sd=2)    # A numeric vector
> round(x, 2)                    # Round to 2 decimal places
> sqrt(abs(x))                   # Square root. Absolute value to avoid sqrt of negative
> log(x + 1)                     # Log (base e). Add 1 to avoid log(0)
> scale(x)                       # Standardize as z-scores
```

The arithmetic functions have no effect on the input data structure x. If you want to transform x you must explicitly assign the returned value back to x. For example:

```
> x = scale(x)   # Standardize x
```

Some arithmetic functions	
round	Round to given number of decimal places
trunc	Truncate down to nearest whole number
ceiling, floor	Round values in a vector up (ceiling) or down (floor)
zapsmall	Replace values in a vector or matrix that are close to zero with 0
abs	Absolute (unsigned) value
sqrt	Square root
exp	Exponential
log, log10, log2	Log to base e, 10, and 2
sin, cos, tan	Trigonometric functions
asin, acos, atan	Inverse (arc) trigonometric functions
scale	Centering and scaling

2.2.2 Descriptive Functions

Descriptive functions take a data structure argument and return a summary. For example a single-valued summary of a vector:

```
> x = rnorm(10, mean=5, sd=2)    # A numeric vector
> length(x)                      # Length (number of elements in x)
> mean(x)                        # Mean of the elements in x
> sd(x)                          # Standard deviation of the elements in x
```

Some summary descriptive functions	
length	Number of elements in a vector
sum	Sum of the values in a vector
min, max, range	Minimum, maximum, and range (min, max) of a vector
mean, median	Mean and median of the values in a vector
sd, var	Standard deviation and variance
cov, cor	Covariance and Pearson correlation

Functions cov and cor return either a single value or a matrix, depending upon the arguments.[23] If the arguments are two vectors a single value is returned. If the argument is a matrix a matrix is returned. The i,j'th element of the matrix is the covariance (using cov) or correlation (using cor) between the i'th and j'th column vectors.

```
> x = rnorm(100)
> y = rnorm(100)
> var(x)
> var(y)              # Variance
> cov(x, y)           # Scalar covariance
> cor(x, y)           # Pearson correlation coefficient
> cov(cbind(x, y))    # Covariance matrix
> cor(cbind(x, y))    # Correlation matrix
```

2.2.3 Operators and Expressions

R has conventional arithmetic expression syntax with the usual arithmetic and conditional operators.[24]

Arithmetic and conditional operators			
x+y	add	x == y	x equal to y?
x−y	subtract	x != y	x not equal to y?
x*y	multiply	x < y	x less than y?
x/y	divide	x <= y	x less than or equal to y?

(continued)

---

[23] Functions are designed where possible to allow different kinds of input data, and to implement the generic meaning of the function in whatever way makes best sense for the kind of data they are given. For example the description of the arguments in help(cor) suggests they can be a numeric vector, matrix or data frame.

[24] See: help(Arithmetic), help(Comparison), and help(Syntax).

(continued)

Arithmetic and conditional operators			
x^y	raise to power	x > y	x greater than y?
x%%y	remainder	x >= y	x greater than or equal to y?
−x	negate		

Vector Arithmetic

The operators are "vectorized" as follows. Unary operators apply element-wise to each cell:

```
> x = c(0, 2, 4, 6, 8, 10)
> − x   # Negate each element
> x^2   # Square each element
```

Binary operators apply element-wise to corresponding pairs of cells:

```
> x = c(0, 2, 4, 6, 8, 10)
> y = c(1, 5, 3, 7, 11, 8)
> x + y   # Add corresponding elements
> x < y   # Test corresponding elements
```

If the vectors are different lengths the shorter vector is "recycled" to match the length of the longer, by concatenating it end-on-end with itself until it is at least as long, trimming excess off the end if necessary.[25] The operation is then applied pair-wise to corresponding cells. The result vector is the same length as the longer argument.

```
> x = c(0, 2, 4, 6, 8, 10)
> y = c(4, 8)
> x + y
> x < y
> x * 4   # Scalar 4 is recycled to match length(x)
> x < 4
```

Matrix Arithmetic

Unary operations and arithmetic functions are applied element-wise. Binary operations are applied between corresponding pairs of elements. Matrices must have the same dimensions to be "conformable" for arithmetic, but if one argument

---

[25] A warning message about fractional recycling is displayed if the length is not an exact multiple. This can safely be ignored, or turned off by the command: options(warn = −1).

is a vector it is recycled to match the length of the matrix. For conventional matrix multiplication[26] use the special operator: %*%. For example:

```
> x = matrix(1:16, nrow=4, ncol=4)
> x^2        # Square each element
> sqrt(x)    # sqrt each element
> x + 0.1    # 0.1 is recycled
> x * x      # Multiply corresponding elements
> x %*% x    # Conventional matrix multiplication
```

Some matrix functions	
t	Transpose
diag	Diagonal
%*%	Inner (dot) product of two vectors $x^t y$, and conventional matrix multiplication
%o%	Outer product of two vectors xy^t
crossprod, tcrossprod	Cross products $x^t y$ and xy^t of matrices
det	Determinant
solve	Inverse
eigen	Eigenvalues and eigenvectors
svd	Singular value decomposition
qr	QR decomposition
chol	Choleski decomposition

Conditional Expressions

Conditional expressions result in logical vectors. The main purpose of these is to represent the vectorized result of a conditional expression so that it can subsequently be applied in conditional indexing.

Conditional operators compare values and return truth values: TRUE or FALSE. For example if x=1 then the conditional expression x > 0 returns the value TRUE.

Conditional operations are defined for numeric, logical, and character vectors. The conditional operators == and != are defined for factors.

Under conditional operations both numerical and logical values are compared numerically.[27] Logical values are treated numerically in this context as: TRUE=>1,

---

[26] Matrix multiplication x %*% y is conformable if ncol(x) == nrow(y). If one argument is a vector it is interpreted as a row or column to suit so a transpose is unnecessary.

[27] Annoyance: when testing for negative numbers an expression like x<-1 will unexpectedly modify x because the <- is interpreted as the assignment operator. The workaround is to include space: x < -1.

FALSE=>0. Character values are compared alphabetically and case-sensitively: the alphabet is in increasing order, for example "ant" < "bee", and upper-case is greater than lower-case so "Ant" > "ant".

Conditional operators are vectorized as follows. When two vectors are compared the shorter is recycled if necessary to make the vectors the same length, then the conditional operation is applied between pairs of corresponding cells. The result is a logical vector the same length as the longer argument. For example:

```
> x = c(2, 4, 6, 8, 10)
> x >= 6      # 6 is recycled to match the length of x
> y = c("apple", "apple", "orange", "apple", "orange")
> y == "apple"
```

Logical vectors can be combined using the operators[28]: & (AND), | (OR), and ! (NOT) to form composite conditions. For example:

```
> x >= 6 & y == "apple"   # TRUE where x >= 6 AND y == "apple"
```

Arithmetic With Logical Vectors

Arithmetic operations are conventional for numeric data. They are not defined for character data. They are defined for logical data by treating logical values as numeric in an arithmetic context as: TRUE=>1 and FALSE=>0.

Consequently the sum function counts TRUE in a logical vector, and the mean function calculates the proportion TRUE. This enables descriptive functions to summarise how a vector meets a given condition. For example

```
> x = c(2, 4, 6, 8, 10)
> y = c("apple", "apple", "orange", "apple", "orange")
> sum(x)                          # Sum of the elements of x
> sum(y)                          # Error! (arithmetic not defined for character data)
> sum(x < 6)                      # How many elements of x are less than 6 (x<6 TRUE)?
> sum(y == "apple")               # How many elements of y are "apple"?
> sum(x = 6 & y == "apple")       # How many x>=6 AND y=="apple"?
> mean(x < 6)                     # What proportion of x is less than 6?
> mean(y == "apple")              # What proportion of y is "apple"?
> mean(x >= 6 & y == "apple")     # What proportion x>=6 AND y=="apple"?
```

---

[28] & and | are vectorized for combining logical index vectors. Corresponding operators && and || result in single truth values, usually for purposes of flow control in a program. See help(Logic, package="base"), and the examples therein which show how to construct truth tables defining the logical operations.

2.3 Factors

Factors represent categorical variables and are used as grouping indicators. The categories are stored internally as numeric codes, with labels to provide meaningful names for each code.

For example a sequence of categorical observations: "apple", "apple","orange","apple","orange" is efficiently stored as numeric codes 1,1,2,1,2. The values of the codes are always restricted to 1,2,...,k, to represent k discrete categories. The labels, here "apple","orange", are a character vector stored with the factor as an attribute named levels. Whenever the factor is used, such as when its value it printed, the labels are mapped onto the codes internally. The order of the labels is important: the first label is mapped to each code 1, the second to each code 2, (and so on if there are more levels). Here "apple" is mapped to each code 1, and "orange" to each code 2.

Use function as.factor to create the factor from a vector, and functions as.numeric and levels to get the factor's internal numeric codes[29] and labels:

```
> x = as.factor(c("apple", "apple", "orange", "apple", "orange"))
> as.numeric(x)   # The internal numeric codes
> levels(x)       # The labels (a character vector)
> x               # Print the value of the factor
```

The factor can be used to indicate which group[30] observations belong to:

	score	condition
1	39	apple
2	14	apple
3	2	orange
4	7	apple
5	44	orange

---

[29] To coerce a factor with numeric labels as a numeric vector first coerce as character using as.character and then as numeric using as.numeric.

[30] There are programming advantages to abstracting the grouping information in this way: it provides a device for manipulating groupings that does not depend upon a particular shape or layout for data, that can accommodate missing observations, and that enables programming easily to express conditions on the groupings, such as to extract and summarise the observations in a particular group.

2.3.1 Making Factors

The read.table function that reads an external text file into a data frame converts columns of non-numeric characters to factors by default. The factor levels depend upon the number of different character strings found in the data.

   Functions as.factor and as.ordered make factors from vectors. Ordered factors[31] differ from factors only in their class. When a vector is converted to a factor the factor labels are the unique values found in the vector by default. Their default order is their natural sort order: alphabetical for character vectors, numerical for numeric vectors.

```
> x = c("orange", "orange", "orange", "orange", "apple")
> as.factor(x)   # Levels in alphabetical order
> x = rep(3:1, each=2)
> as.factor(x)   # Levels in numerical order
```

Function gl (generate levels) is used to make grouping factors for balanced experimental designs. Use function rep to add replications to the grouping factor if necessary.

```
> gl(3, 10, labels=c("low", "med", "high"))   # Grouping factor
```

Function cut makes a factor from a numeric vector by dividing the numeric range into intervals to group the values. The interval boundaries are specified using an argument named breaks. By default the intervals are defined as "open on the left", (or equivalently "closed on the right"), and are indicated by labels like (...]. This means values that fall on a break between intervals will be grouped to the left of the break. Any value on the left break of the left-most interval is classified as NA, (since there is no information about the interval to the left of that). Set argument include.lowest=TRUE to override this behaviour and group such values within the lowest interval. Set argument right=FALSE to re-define the intervals so that values on a break are grouped to the right of the break. (In that case include.lowest=TRUE groups right-most values within the highest interval). For example:

---

[31] An ordered factor does not refer to the order of the level labels, but simply marks the factor as "ordered" so it can be handled appropriately by functions where the distinction between nominal and ordinal data is relevant. For example the contrast coding used in linear modelling functions has different defaults for unordered and ordered factors. Unordered factors get comparisons between group means. Ordered factors get trend analysis.

```
> x = c(20, 21, 30, 39, 40)
> cut(x, breaks=c(20, 30, 40))                    # Open on the left
> cut(x, breaks=c(20, 30, 40), inc=TRUE)
> cut(x, breaks=c(20, 30, 40), right=FALSE)   # Open on the right
> cut(x, breaks=c(20, 30, 40), right=FALSE, inc=TRUE)
```

The breaks can be specified as a single number (greater than 1) giving the number of intervals. The quantile function is useful for calculating breaks so that the intervals will contain equal frequencies of values. For example:

```
> x = round(rexp(1000)*100)
> hist(x)
> g1 = cut(x, breaks=4, inc=TRUE)    # Breaks at equal intervals
> g2 = cut(x, breaks=quantile(x), inc=TRUE)   # Breaks at quantiles
> table(g1)
> table(g2)   # Quantile intervals try to contain equal frequencies
```

2.3.2 Operations on Factors

Some functions for working with factors	
as.factor, factor	Make a factor from a vector
as.ordered, ordered	Make an ordered factor from a vector
gl	Make a factor by generating (equal sized) levels
cut	Make a factor by cutting a vector at given break points
relevel	Set the first (reference) level of a factor
as.numeric	Get a factor's numeric codes
levels	Get the labels of a factor's levels
nlevels	Get the number of levels of a factor
:, interaction	Cross-classify factors

Arithmetic operators are not valid for factors. The conditional operators == and != are valid for factors and typically are used for conditional indexing in a vector or data frame. The : operator between two factors of the same length returns a factor by cross-classifying its arguments. The result is a factor with levels made from all combinations of the levels of the arguments.

```
> g1 = gl(2, 6, labels=c(" + ", " − "))
> g2 = gl(3, 4, labels=c("A", "B", "C"))
> g1:g2                # Cross-classify the factors
> nlevels(g1:g2)       # Number of levels in the crossing (2×3)
```

2.3.3 Re-ordering and Re-labelling

Functions factor and ordered make factors from vectors, in the same way as as.factor and as.ordered. They have additional arguments to control the labels which, given a factor instead of a vector as input, can be used to re-order and re-label the factor's levels.

The levels argument specifies an order[32] for the labels in terms of the current labels. When the labels are re-ordered the corresponding numeric codes are changed as well to preserve the mapping between labels and codes. The labels argument specifies new values for the labels, which are re-labelled in the order given. When both levels and labels are given the new labels re-label the old in their order specified by levels.

```
> x = as.factor(c("orange", "orange", "apple", "orange", "apple", "pear"))
> factor(x, levels=c("orange", "pear", "apple"))   # Re-order
> factor(x, labels=c("A", "O", "P"))               # Re-label
> factor(x, levels=c("orange", "pear", "apple"), labels=c("O", "P", "A"))
```

2.4 Indexing

There are functions that return the first and last few parts of a data structure, (head and tail), and there is a rudimentary editor GUI for data frames (fix and edit). But indexing is a more powerful approach to data manipulation in general.

Objects have distinct parts: the rows and columns of a data frame, the components of a list, the individual cells within a vector, matrix, array, or data frame. These parts are ordered and numbered, and may also have names associated with them. Indexing means accessing parts by name or by number to extract or replace values.[33] The index can be conditional and derived programmatically, (for example to extract or replace "scores for males aged over 50 and in employment").

---

[32] The order is relevant to the default appearance of tables and graphs, and also in modelling functions when a reference level is used for comparisons. See also function relevel to re-order levels so a given level is the first (reference) level.

[33] See: help(Extract), help("[.data.frame"), and help(subset).

2.4.1 Indexing by Name

Objects may have a names attribute to associate a label with each part.[34] For example the names of a data frame are its column names, most often representing the names of variables. The names of a list are the names of the objects collected in the list.

An object's names can be accessed using the names function, and then its parts can be accessed by name using a $ syntax. For example, the provided data set named sleep consists of two variables in a data frame:

```
> names(sleep)        # Names of the variables in data frame 'sleep'
> sleep$extra         # Access variable 'extra' in data frame 'sleep'
> mean(sleep$extra)   # Mean of 'extra' in data frame 'sleep'
```

Many functions return multi-valued results as a single object with named components. Individual parts of the results can be extracted by name. For example:

```
> x = t.test(extra~group, data=sleep, paired=TRUE)   # Paired t-test
> names(x)   # The names of the components returned by 't.test'
> x$p.value  # The p value from the t test
```

Attaching Data Frames

In situations where the $ syntax is cumbersome, functions attach and detach can be used to enable access to the columns of a data frame as if they are variables outside the data frame.[35]

```
> attach(sleep)   # Attach a data frame
> mean(extra)     # Access variables by name
> detach(sleep)   # Detach the data frame
```

Functions with and transform provide temporary access to data frame columns by name. Function with enables evaluation with data frame variables. Function transform enables evaluation in the data frame and returns the transformed data frame. For example:

---

[34] See: help(names), and also help(colnames), help(dimnames), and help(row.names).

[35] Caveat: assignments to attached variables are not assignments to the data frame. Attaching a data frame works by inserting the object on the search path so the variables within the data frame can be found by name. See help(search). However the global environment is always searched first, so variables in the data frame may be masked by variables in the global environment. Any assignment to variables of the same name assigns in the global environment and not in the data frame. So assignments to attached variables have no effect on the data frame.

```
> with(sleep, mean(extra))              # Mean of 'extra' in data frame 'sleep'
> transform(sleep, ctime=scale(extra))  # Add a derived variable
```

2.4.2 Indexing by Number

The parts of an object, (the rows and columns of a data frame, the components of a list, the individual cells within a vector, matrix, array, or data frame), are ordered and numbered. The numbering always starts with 1, (not 0), and ends at the length or dimensions of the object.

The length of an object, (for example the number of cells in a vector, or the number of components in a list), is returned by function length:

```
> length(c("x", "y", "z"))   # Length of a vector
```

The dimensions of an object, (such as the number of rows and columns in a matrix or data frame), are returned by functions dim, nrow and ncol. For example, using the provided data set named swiss:

```
> dim(swiss)    # Dimensions (rows, columns) of data frame 'swiss'
> nrow(swiss)   # Number of rows in data frame 'swiss'
> ncol(swiss)   # Number of columns in data frame 'swiss'
```

The syntax for indexing by number uses square brackets. For example to index the cells of a vector by number:

```
> x = c("x", "y", "z")
> x[1]                  # Get the first cell (x[0] is undefined)
> x[length(x)]          # Get the last cell
> x[1] = "a"            # Set the first cell
```

A feature of R is that the indices are vectors, enabling simultaneous access to a slice or subset of cells. The result is the same length as the index vector, (which may be longer than the object being indexed). The index addresses particular cells by number and these are returned in the order given in the index. This enables repetition, re-ordering, and sorting.

```
> x[1:2]                    # Get the first two cells
> x[c(3, 1)]                # Get cells 3 and 1 in that order
> x[c(rep(3, 4), rep(1, 3))]  # Get cell 3 (4 times) and 1 (3 times)
> x[1:2] = c("p", "q")      # Set the first two cells
```

Vectors have a single index, as in: x[i]. Matrix and data frame cells have pairs of indices, respectively for rows and columns, as in: x[i,j]. Arrays have tuples of indices depending on the dimensionality of the array, as in: x[i,j,k]

(for a 3-dimensional array). An empty index is shorthand for a complete index.
For example:

```
> swiss[c(10, 15), 2:3]    # Index rows 10 and 15, and columns 2 to 3
> swiss[c(10, 15),]        # Rows 10, 15 and all columns (empty column index)
> swiss[, 2:3]             # Columns 2:3 and all rows (empty row index)
```

If the object has named parts an index vector can be character or numeric:

```
> swiss[c(10, 15), c("Agriculture", "Examination")]   # Same as: swiss[c(10, 15), 2:3]
```

A single index to a data frame accesses columns by number or by name. Names
can for example be derived using grep to find names matching a pattern, (useful
when the data frame has hundreds of columns). The columns are returned as a data
frame, or a single column can be returned in its native type using double brackets.
For example:

```
> swiss[2:3]             # Columns 2:3, (same as swiss[, 2:3])
> swiss[3]              # Column 3 returned as a data frame
> swiss[[3]]            # Column 3 returned as a vector
> swiss["Examination"]  # Column 3 accessed by name
```

2.4.3 Inserting and Deleting Rows or Columns

Numeric indices in R can be positive or negative, (the elements of an index vector
must either be all positive or all negative). A negative index accesses all the cells
NOT indexed. This can be used to delete cells, rows, or columns. For example to
delete rows or columns of a data frame (assign the results if you wish to save
them):

```
> swiss[-c(3, 5, 7),]    # Drop rows 3, 5, and 7
> swiss[-6]              # Drop column 6
```

A data frame can dynamically be increased in size with new rows or columns,[36]
either by name (using $ syntax) or by index number. For example:

```
> swiss$zFertility = scale(swiss$Fertility)   # Append a derived variable
> sleep$zFertility = NULL                      # Drop a variable by name
> swiss[nrow(swiss)+1,] = NA                   # Append a row (of NA values)
> swiss = swiss[-nrow(swiss),]                 # Delete a row
```

---

[36] Columns may only be appended. A new column is not allowed to leave "holes" after existing
columns.

To insert a row or column use rbind and cbind to construct the data frame around the insert. For example:

```
> rbind(swiss[1:6,], NA, swiss[7:nrow(swiss),])   # Insert 7th row
> cbind(swiss[1:2], NA, swiss[3:ncol(swiss)])      # Insert 3rd column
```

2.4.4 Indexing with Factors

Factors can be indexed[37] by numeric or logical vectors, and can be assigned values provided these are amongst the factor's labels:

```
> g = as.factor(c("orange", "orange", "apple", "orange", "apple", "pear"))
> g[4]
> g[4] = "apple"
```

A factor can be used as an index vector, and then its numeric codes are the index.

```
> x = c("red", "orange", "green", "yellow")
> x[g]
```

The conditionals == and != are valid for factors and the resulting logical vector is typically used to index a vector or data frame. For example:

```
> x = 1:6
> x[g=="apple"]   # Get values of x where factor g is "apple"
```

Indexing can be used to merge or drop factor levels

```
> factor(c("apple", "orange", "orange")[g])   # Merge levels
> g[g!="pear"]                                 # Subset the factor
> g[g!="pear", drop=TRUE]                      # Drop a level
> factor(g, levels=c(levels(g), "lemon"))      # Add a level
```

2.4.5 Conditional Indexing

Conditioning by String Pattern Matching

The grep function is used to extract elements of character vectors by string pattern matching using regular expressions. By default it returns the numeric index of each match, or with argument value=TRUE it returns the matching elements

---

[37] See: help("[.factor").

themselves. For example to extract a subset of variables from a data frame by
matching name patterns:

```
> swiss[grep("^E", names(swiss))]   # Variables with names beginning "E..."
```

Indexing with Logical Vectors

Conditional indexing means indexing with a logical vector that has been derived
from a conditional expression. For example:

```
> i = swiss$Agriculture > 50 & swiss$Education > 8
```

A conditional expression returns a logical vector. Logical index vectors are
different from other kinds of index. Numeric and character index vectors address
particular cells by number or by name, and these are returned in the order given in
the index. Logical index vectors specify a pattern of cells to be addressed. If
necessary the pattern is recycled so that the index vector matches the length of the
object being indexed. The index is then applied element-wise and addresses cells
corresponding to cells of the logical vector that are TRUE.

```
> swiss[i, ]                        # Index rows where the condition is TRUE
> swiss[!i, ]                       # Index rows where the condition is NOT TRUE
> mean(swiss[i, "Fertility"])       # Mean 'Fertility' within condition
```

Some functions for logical and set operations	
any	TRUE if any of the arguments contains TRUE
all	TRUE if all of the arguments are TRUE
which	Get numeric indices where a logical vector is TRUE
grep, agrep	Get indices or values that match regular expression patterns
union	Set union, (elements in vector x OR y or both)
intersect	Set intersection, (elements in vector x AND y)
x %in% y	Get vector containing TRUE for each element of x that is also in y
unique	Get vector of unique values by dropping duplicate values
duplicated	Get vector containing TRUE to indicate duplicated values
upper.tri	TRUE for the upper-triangle of a matrix
lower.tri	TRUE for the lower-triangle of a matrix

2.4.6 Sorting

There is a function rev that reverses a vector's order, and a function sort sorts a
vector numerically or alphabetically into ascending or descending order. A more
flexible approach is to sort by deriving and applying an appropriate index vector.

The benefit of this two-step approach is that it enables you sort one vector by another or, for example, to sort the rows of a data frame by one or more of the columns.

The function `order` is used to derive the index vector that would sort a vector. For example the first element of `order(x)` is the index of the lowest-valued element in x. The next is the index of the next lowest value, and so on:

```
> x = c(2, 4, 1, 3)
> order(x)
> x[order(x)]   # Sort x using an ordered index vector
```

An appropriately ordered index vector can be used to sort the rows or columns of a data frame:

```
> # Sort rows of 'swiss' by 'Examination'
> swiss[order(swiss$Examination),]
> # Sort rows of 'swiss' by 'Examination' and within that by 'Education'
> swiss[order(swiss$Examination, swiss$Education),]
> # Sort columns of 'swiss' by name
> swiss[, order(names(swiss))]
```

2.5 Reshaping

Reshaping data frames	
stack, unstack	Stack or unstack columns to reshape into long or wide format
reshape	Reshape a data frame into long or wide format
merge	Merge data frames by common column or row names

One purpose of reshaping a data frame is to convert between "long format" and "wide format". A "long format" data frame has one column for each variable. A "wide format" data frame has one row for each subject or case. These formats are different when there are repeated measures of subjects in time.

In long format a time-varying variable is a single column containing all the subjects measures of that variable at all time-points. The data frame must then also have factors to indicate which subject and which time-point each measure belongs to.

In wide format a time-varying variable is spread over several columns, one for each time-point. In that case it is clear which subject and time-point each measure

belongs to from its location in the data frame. However the data must be balanced
in the sense that all subjects have a complete set of measures at all time-points,
otherwise it is necessary to pad the data with missing values to preserve the
rectangular shape of the data frame. One advantage of long format is that grouping
factors can represent unbalanced data.

2.5.1 Stacking and Unstacking

The basic operation of reshaping is stacking and unstacking. The stack function
takes a data frame and stacks its columns into a single column, returning this in a
data frame as a column named values, with a factor named ind to indicate which
of the original columns each value belongs to. For example, stack the four iris
measures:

```
> stack(iris[1:4])
```

The unstack function takes a column and unstacks it into several columns by
splitting it on a factor. It returns a data frame if the factor is balanced, or a list if
not.[38] To check balance the replications function counts the number of replications, and it too returns a list if the groups are unbalanced. For both functions the
name of the column and the grouping factor are specified using a formula. For
example with the sleep data:

```
> replications(extra~group, sleep)    # Balanced data (10 reps per group)
> unstack(sleep, extra~group)         # Data frame (unstack 'extra' by 'group')
```

As an example of unbalanced data, the ChickWeight data contains repeated
measures of 50 chickens weight at several time-points. Different chickens were
measured different numbers of times:

```
> replications(weight~Chick, ChickWeight)   # Unbalanced data
> unstack(ChickWeight, weight~Chick)        # List (unstack 'weight' by 'Chick')
```

2.5.2 Reshaping: Wide and Long

The reshape function is a more general reshaping tool[39] designed for data that are
repeated measures of subjects in time. It has arguments to specify the time-varying

---

[38] See also functions split and unsplit which split a vector or data frame into a list, or
combine list components.
[39] See also functions melt and cast in package reshape.

variables in a data frame that are to be stacked or unstacked. It handles unbalanced data by inserting NA as appropriate, and also treats time-invariant variables appropriately.

For example to reshape the ChickWeight data from long to wide, use argument v.names to specify the time-varying variable to be unstacked, and arguments idvar and timevar to specify the subject and time-point factors:

```
> dat = reshape(ChickWeight, direction="wide", v.names="weight",
+                idvar="Chick", timevar="Time")
```

The result contains NA because the data are not balanced. The result also includes the Diet variable, a time-invariant variable that was simply repeated at each time-point in long format.

To reshape from wide to long, use argument varying to specify the columns to be stacked, and argument v.names to specify a name for the stacked column. For example if the four iris measures are taken as four time-points with measures of one time-varying variable:

```
> reshape(iris, direction="long", varying=1:4, v.names="value")
```

The reshape function allows more than one time-varying variable. For example if the four iris measures are taken as two time-varying variables, each with measures at two time-points iris[1:2] and iris[3:4]:

```
> reshape(iris, direction="long", varying=list(1:2,3:4),
+         v.names=c("value1", "value2"))
```

2.5.3 Merging

The merge function performs a database "join" operation between two data frames based on columns that contain values common to both data frames. For example if two data frames both have a column named id containing some values common to both data frames, the merge function returns a data frame by joining rows with matching id:

```
> x = data.frame(id=1:10, var1=1:10)
> y = data.frame(id=3:7, var2=letters[3:7])
> merge(x, y, by="id")
```

The default behaviour is to return a data frame that contains just the rows that are common to both input data frames, that is rows where the input data frames have the same value in the by variable. This can be overridden using logical arguments all.x and all.y. For example if all.x=TRUE the returned data frame will have all the rows from x, (the first input data frame), whether they match in y or not. Rows that don't match in y are then given NA values in the columns merged from y. For example:

```
> merge(x, y, by="id", all.x=TRUE)   # All rows from x
> merge(x, y, by="id", all.y=TRUE)   # All rows from y
```

2.6 Missing Values

The special value NA ("Not Available") is used to represent a missing value. The NA value can appear in a vector of any type without coercion.

2.6.1 Recoding Missing Values

Many R functions understand NA in the sense that they have built-in methods for handling NA values. Missing values should be coded as NA to take advantage of these.

Function read.table recodes blanks as NA by default. Other missing value codes can be passed to argument na.strings. For example to recode all . or −999 as NA:

```
> read.table("data.txt", na.strings=c(".", "−999"))
```

2.6.2 Operations with Missing Values

If any data are missing the general principle is that it is better by default to propagate a missing value code than an incorrect summary or result. A missing value can be caught and handled by subsequent processes. An incorrect result might slip through un-noticed. This principle applies logically to arithmetic and conditional operations. Any operation involving NA is undecidable and so the only sensible result is NA. Descriptive functions by default will propagate NA values rather than a potentially incorrect summary. For example:

```
> x = c(3.14, NA, 2.72, 1.96)
> y = c(NA, 2.72, 1.96, 3.14)
> mean(x)
> cor(x, y)
> cor(cbind(x, y))   # The default use="everything"
> sum(x==NA)         # NOT the way to count NA
```

2.6.3 Counting and Sorting Missing Values

A special function is.na is needed to test for NA. The function returns TRUE where its argument is NA.

```
> x = c(3.14, 0, NA, 1)
> is.na(x)              # Test for NA
> sum(is.na(x))         # Count NA
```

Function complete.cases is provided for testing for NA along data frame rows. Other functions provide arguments to accommodate NA. For example:

```
> dat = data.frame(A=c(1, 0, NA, 0, NA), B=c(NA, 1, 0, 1, 0))   # Data frame with some NA
> sum(complete.cases(dat))           # Count complete cases
> sum(!complete.cases(dat))          # Count incomplete cases
> summary(dat)                       # Summary counts NA by column
> table(dat, useNA="always")         # Cross-tabulate including NA
> dat[order(dat$A),]                 # Sort by column A with NA last
> dat[order(dat$A, na.last=F),]      # Sort by column A with NA first
```

2.6.4 Handling Missing Values

Cases with missing values can be dropped altogether:

```
> dat = dat[complete.cases(dat),]   # Drop cases (rows) with any NA
```

It is possible to impute[40] values that are missing. Descriptive and modelling functions have default methods for handling NA values and generally provide arguments to override the default behaviour and specify how NA is handled.

Descriptive functions (such as sum, mean, sd, and so forth) propagate NA by default but provide an argument named na.rm ("NA remove") that can be set to TRUE to instruct the function to omit all NA from the calculation. Functions cov and cor have a use argument that can be set as use="complete.obs" for casewise deletion (aka listwise deletion), and use="pairwise.complete.obs" to use all complete pairs of observations in the calculation.

---

[40] See package mvnmle for maximum likelihood imputation, and various packages for multiple imputation such as mitools and mice listed at http://cran.r-project.org/web/views/Multivariate.html.

```
> x = c(3.14, NA, 2.72, 1.96)
> y = c(NA, 2.72, 1.96, 3.14)
> mean(x, na.rm=TRUE)
> cor(x, y, use="pairwise.complete.obs")
> cor(cbind(x, y), use="pairwise.complete.obs")
```

Modelling functions (such as lm, aov, glm, and so forth), and other functions for multivariate analysis (such as princomp, prcomp, and factanal), have an argument named na.action which is set to the name of a function to handle incomplete data. The default setting is the function named na.omit which handles missing values by casewise deletion. If instead you wish to propagate NA values to fitted values, residuals, predicted values, or factor scores, preserving the length of these data,[41] then it is necessary to set na.action=na.exclude.

```
> fitted(lm(y~x))                          # NA omitted from result
> fitted(lm(y~x, na.action=na.exclude))    # NA preserved in result
```

2.7 Mapping Functions

R provides the usual facilities for programming loops for iterations,[42] but in practice you seldom need to use them. Use mapping functions instead because they are faster and easier to program. These are functions that apply (map) a given function over parts of a data structure. Several mapping functions are provided for different kinds of data structure and groupings.

Mapping functions	
apply	Map a function to the margins (rows or columns) of an array
sapply, lapply	Map a function to each cell of a vector, column of a data frame, or component of a list
replicate	Repeated evaluation of an expression
tapply	Map a function to a vector grouped by one or more factors
mapply	Map a multivariate function to corresponding cells of multiple vectors, columns of multiple data frames, or components of multiple lists
outer	Map a binary function to corresponding elements of two matrices
aggregate, by	Map a function to data frame columns grouped by one or more factors

---

[41] See: help(na.fail) and help(naresid). Note that na.exclude works by passing a message, via the result's na.action attribute, to functions that subsequently process the result. To take advantage of na.exclude it is necessary to process the result with an appropriate function. For example fitted(fit) and residuals(fit) propagate NA values, but fit$fitted and fit$residuals do not.

[42] See: help(Control).

2.7.1 Repeated Evaluation

The replicate function is often used in conjunction with sample for resampling and permutations[43]:

```
> x = c("bob", "carol", "ted", "alice")
> replicate(24, sample(x))   # Permute x 24 times
```

2.7.2 Applying Functions

Functions are provided for calculating row and column sums and means of a data frame. Functions colSums and colMeans calculate column sums and means, and functions rowSums and rowMeans calculate row sums and means. Function rowsum calculates column sums over rows grouped by a factor. Mapping functions[44] allow arbitrary functions to be applied.

Use sapply to map a function to each column of a data frame. For example the provided iris data set:

```
> sapply(iris, class)      # Apply class to columns of iris
> sapply(iris[1:4], mean)  # Apply mean to columns 1:4
```

Use tapply to map a function to subsets of a vector grouped by one or more factors. Pass multiple factor arguments within a list. For example the provided warpbreaks data set:

```
> attach(warpbreaks)
> tapply(breaks, tension, mean)
> tapply(breaks, list(wool, tension), mean)   # Factor arguments within a list
> detach(warpbreaks)
```

Instead of attaching the data frame to facilitate access to the variables you may prefer to use with:

```
> with(warpbreaks, tapply(breaks, list(wool, tension), mean))   # Using with
```

Functions by and aggregate both map a given function to subsets of data frame columns grouped by one or more factors. They differ in that function by returns a list, and function aggregate returns a data frame. Function by is oriented towards extracting more complicated information from each group, such as

---

[43] See also: combn to generate combinations of elements, choose for the number of combinations, and factorial for the size of a full permutation. See permutations in package gtools for enumerating a full permutation.

[44] See: apropos("apply").

model fits, and returning these in a form that can subsequently be processed using sapply.[45] Function aggregate is oriented towards computing summary statistics for each group, and returning these in a form that can more easily be combined into a table using cbind.

```
> by(iris[1:4], list(iris$Species), mean)
> aggregate(iris[1:4], list(iris$Species), mean)
```

Passing Arguments to the Mapped Function

Mapping functions that have an argument named "..." allow additional optional arguments to be passed to the mapped function. For example it is often necessary to pass the argument na.rm=TRUE to a summary descriptive function to omit missing values from the calculation.

```
> sapply(iris[1:4], mean, na.rm=TRUE)
> sapply(iris[1:4], mean, na.rm=TRUE, trim=0.2)   # Trimmed mean
```

2.8 Writing Functions

Custom functions to extend the R language can be created using the function keyword.[46] For example a function to calculate the standard error of a sample vector x could be defined as follows:

```
> se = function(x) {
+       sd(x)/sqrt(length(x))
+ }
```

The function arguments are declared as the arguments to the function keyword. Here there is just one argument, named x. The calculations performed by the function is defined in the function's body between {...}. The value returned by the function is the value of its final line.[47] The name of the function is the name of the variable you assign it to. Here the function is named se. This function could then be used as follows:

```
> y = rnorm(100)
> se(y)      # Call the se function, passing argument y
```

---

[45] See the examples in help(by).

[46] See: help("function").

[47] See also: help(return).

The function can be mapped to a data structure in the same way as any provided function, for example:

```
> sapply(iris[1:4], se)   # Apply function se to columns 1:4
```

2.8.1 Anonymous Functions

If the custom function is a small one-off function it is typically defined at the place it is used as an "anonymous" function, (a function with no name). For example:

```
> sapply(iris[1:4], function(x) sd(x)/sqrt(length(x)))   # Anonymous se
> sapply(iris[1:4], function(x) sum(is.na(x)))           # Count NA
```

2.8.2 Optional Arguments

Optional arguments and their default values are declared as name=value in the argument list. Argument checking within the function can be reported by function stop (for fatal errors) or warning (for non-fatal warning messages).

For example a function to calculate the small sample confidence interval for the mean, and return a list containing the lower and upper limits:

```
> ci = function(x, conf=0.95) {
+        if(length(x)<2) stop("Not enough \'x\' observations")
+        y = t.test(x, conf.level=conf)$conf.int
+        list(lower=y[1], upper=y[2])
+ }
> # Using the function:
> y = rnorm(100)
> ci(y)                       # 95% CI
> ci(y, conf=0.99)            # 99% CI
```

A special argument '...' is used to pass arguments on to function calls within a function. For example:

```
> ci = function(x,...) {
+        if(length(x) < 2) stop("Not enough \'x\' observations")
+        y = t.test(x,...)$conf.int
+        list(lower=y[1], upper=y[2])
+ }
> ci(y, conf.level=0.99)   # 99% CI
```

Chapter 3
Tables and Graphs

Abstract Creating tables and plotting graphs.

Keywords Tables · Descriptives · Results · Base graphics · lattice graphics

3.1 Tables

Working with tables	
dimnames	Get or set table dimension names
ftable	Print "flat" table
xtabs	Data frame to array
as.data.frame.table	Array to data frame
table	Cross tabulations and contingency tables
prop.table	Scale table cells as proportions
margin.table	Get marginal sums
addmargins	Add row and/or column margins by a function

M. Allerhand, *A Tiny Handbook of R*, SpringerBriefs in Statistics,
DOI: 10.1007/978-3-642-17980-8_3, © Springer-Verlag Berlin Heidelberg 2011

3.1.1 Frequency Tables

Tables are arrays[1] of cells containing values of the same type. Use function dim to
get the dimensions of a table, and dimnames to get its labels.[2]

For example, the provided HairEyeColor data set is a 3-dimensional table containing counts of the hair colour, eye colour, and sex of a sample of statistics students.

```
> dim(HairEyeColor)          # Dimensions of the table
> dimnames(HairEyeColor)     # Dimension names (labels)
```

Tables with 1 or 2 dimensions are displayed as 1 or 2-way layouts of cells.
Tables with more than 2 dimensions are displayed as a list of 2-D sub-tables. The
ftable function is provided to format such tables for display as "flat" tables. The
function has arguments named row.vars and col.vars to specify which
dimensions appears as rows or columns, by index number or dimension name.

```
> HairEyeColor               # A list of sub-tables

> ftable(HairEyeColor)       # Format as a flat table

> ftable(HairEyeColor, row.vars=2, col.vars=c(3, 1))
```

Tables are indexed as arrays, in the same way as vectors and matrices, with an
index for each dimension[3] of the table. The data structure can be subsetted or
re-organised by indexing. To extract a particular 2-D sub-table leave two indices
empty. For example to extract the hair colour by eye colour sub-tables:

```
> HairEyeColor[, , 1]   # Sex=="Male"
> HairEyeColor[, , 2]   # Sex=="Female"
```

Tables that contain counts can be aggregated by summing cells. Use apply to
sum over sub-tables:

```
> apply(HairEyeColor, 1, sum)        # Sum all Hair
> apply(HairEyeColor, 2, sum)        # Sum all Eye
> apply(HairEyeColor, c(1, 2), sum)  # Sum all Hair by Eye
```

Table data can be stored in a data frame instead of an array.[4] For example
counts may be stored in a single column, alongside several factor columns to

---

[1] The array data structure is a multi-dimensional layout of cells. Vectors and matrices are the
1-D and 2-D cases. Arrays enable tables that are not limited to 1-D and 2-D layouts, but may
represent groupings in several dimensions.

[2] Table labels are called "dimnames" (dimension names, the names along each dimension), and
"dnn" (dimnames names, the names of the dimensions).

[3] Array dimensions are referred to as "margins" in the documentation, meaning a generalization
of "row" or "column".

[4] Arrays are compact and relatively easy to subset and reshape. They are not so easy to combine.
(But see package abind). Data frames are easier to combine or merge, (see: c, cbind, rbind,
merge).

indicate which table cell each count belongs to. The levels of these factors correspond to the "dimnames" of the array.

Use functions as.data.frame.table and xtabs[5] to convert between array and data frame representations:

```
> x=as.data.frame.table(HairEyeColor)   # Array to data frame
> xtabs(Freq~., x)                       # Data frame to array
```

Count data in frequency-weighted format in a data frame can be converted to raw count data by repeating each row by its frequency:

```
> x=x[rep(1:nrow(x), x$Freq), 1:3]   # Raw count data
```

Cross Tabulation

Functions table and xtabs return objects structured as arrays of class "table".[6] The table function creates a frequency table from one or more factors given as arguments. With more than one factor, table creates a cross-tabulation which is a contingency table of cells containing the count of each combination of factor levels.[7]

```
> table(x$Hair)               # Count of each Hair colour
> table(x$Hair, x$Eye)        # Cross-tab of Hair by Eye
> table(x$Hair, x$Eye, x$Sex) # Cross-tab of Hair by Eye by Sex
```

The table labels can be set or changed using dimnames:

```
> tab=table(x$Hair, x$Eye)   # 2-D table
> dimnames(tab)              # Get the dimnames
> # Set dnn (dimnames names) only:
> names(dimnames(tab))=c("Hair colour", "Eye colour")
> # Set dimnames only:
> dimnames(tab)=list(c("A", "B", "C", "D"), c("E", "F", "G", "H"))
> # Set both dnn and dimnames:
> dimnames(tab)=list(hair=c("A", "B", "C", "D"), eye=c("E", "F", "G", "H"))
```

---

[5] xtabs uses a formula argument to specify which variable in the data frame contains the frequencies, and which variables are the grouping factors. In the formula the frequency variable is specified on the left side of the tilde, and the grouping factors separated by + signs are specified on the right. Alternatively a . on the right side can be used to specify all the variables in the data frame except the frequency variable denoted on the left side. The left side of the formula can be empty, in which case the frequency of each cell is assumed to be 1.

[6] The main purpose of having a separate class "table" is to enable the generic summary function to select a method to carry out a chi-squared test for independence of factors, given a table object. See: help(table).

[7] table omits NA by default. Set argument useNA="ifany" to include a count of NA.

Proportions and Percentages

Frequency tables can be converted to tables of proportions or percentages using function prop.table. Summary statistics can be added in the table margins using function addmargins.[8] The table data can be rounded to a given number of decimal places using function round.

```
> tab=table(x$Hair, x$Eye)                    # 2-D table
> prop.table(tab, margin=1)                   # Proportions of each row sum
> round(prop.table(tab, margin=1)*100, 2)     # ... as percentages, rounded
> addmargins(round(prop.table(tab, margin=1)*100, 2), margin=2)
```

3.1.2 Tables of Cell Means and Other Summaries

The tapply function maps a given function to groups of a vector split on one or more factors. If the vector is split on more than one factor, the factors must be passed as a single list argument. For example a table of cell means using the warpbreaks data:

```
> with(warpbreaks, tapply(breaks, tension, mean))              # one factor
> with(warpbreaks, tapply(breaks, list(tension, wool), mean))  # two factors
```

Any function can be applied, for example instead of mean use var for a table of cell variances. Additional arguments may be passed to the mapped function through the tapply "..." argument. For example:

```
> with(warpbreaks, tapply(breaks, list(tension, wool), mean, na.rm=TRUE))
```

Functions that make tables of descriptives are provided by other packages. For example function describe in package psych:

```
> library(psych)
> describe(iris[1:4])
> describe(iris[1:4])[c("n", "mean", "sd", "skew", "kurtosis")]
```

---

[8] prop.table uses a margin argument to specify which margin (which dimension of the table) to calculate along. For example in a 2-D table margin=1 specifies calculations along each row, and margin=2 specifies calculations down each column. The addmargins function uses the margin argument to specify which margin to add to the table. In a 2-D table margin=1 adds a row margin, (at the foot of the table), margin=2 adds a column margin (on the right of the table). addmargins calculates marginal sums by default. For alternative summaries pass a function, for example mean, to the FUN argument.

Complicated tables can be made by combining tables using function abind.[9] For example a table with multiple statistics of multiple variables split on a grouping factor.

```
> library(psych)      # For 'describe.by'
> library(abind)      # For 'abind'
> a=describe.by(iris[1:4], iris$Species)
> a=abind(a, along=0)
> ftable(a, col.vars=3)
```

Tables may be converted to data frames and combined using rbind and cbind. This would be necessary if the tables are to contain both numeric and character data, some columns of numbers and some columns of names.

3.1.3 Saving Tables

The simplest way to save tables, or any printed output from R, is to use the sink function to divert output to a file in the current working folder.

```
> sink("myresults.txt", split=T)   # Save R console output
> # ...any printed output here is diverted to the file...
> sink()                           # ...turn off saving
```

Use function write.table to write tables, matrices, or data frames to a file in the current working folder.[10] Use function write.ftable for flat tables created by ftable.

```
> tab=with(warpbreaks, tapply(breaks, list(tension, wool), mean))
> tab=round(tab, 2)
> write.table(tab, file="tab.txt", sep='\t', col.names=NA, quote=F)
> write.table(tab, file="tab.csv", sep=", ", col.names=NA, quote=F)
> write.ftable(ftable(tab), file="tab.txt", quote=F)
```

Use function xtable in package xtable to generate a LaTeX table (Tables 3.1 and 3.2).[11]

---

[9] Function abind is in package abind, and is designed to combine arrays. If arrays are combined using c it strips the dim and dimnames attributes which are required by ftable.

[10] A saved .txt file opens in Notepad. A .csv file opens in MS Excel.

[11] See: help(Sweave).

```
> library(xtable)
> tab1=with(warpbreaks, table(tension, wool))
> tab2=round(with(warpbreaks, tapply(breaks, list(tension, wool), mean)), 2)
> xtable(tab1, caption="Frequency")
```

Table 3.1 Frequency

	A	B
L	9	9
M	9	9
H	9	9

```
> xtable(tab2, caption="Cell means")
```

Table 3.2 Cell means

	A	B
L	44.56	28.22
M	24.00	28.78
H	24.56	18.78

3.2 Graphs

The original R graphics package is referred to as "base graphics". Other graphics packages include lattice and ggplot2.

3.2.1 Base Graphics

The concept of the base graphics functions is for successive functions to add graphics and build plots up. This lead to two kinds of functions: "high-level" functions that create new graphs with axes, labels and titles, and "low-level" functions that annotate plots, adding points, lines, and text. Create a new graph using a high-level function, and use successive low-level functions to add further graphics if necessary.

High Level Graphics

High level graphics	
plot	Scatterplot
pairs	Scatterplot matrix
coplot	Conditioning plot
hist	Histogram

(continued)

(continued)

High level graphics	
stem	Stem-and-leaf plot
boxplot	Box-and-whisker plot
qqnorm	Quantile-quantile plot
barplot	Bar plot
dotchart	Dot plot
interaction.plot	Profile plot of group means

Distribution plots:

```
> x=iris$Petal.Length
> hist(x)
> plot(density(x))
> stem(x)
> qqnorm(x)
> boxplot(iris[3:4])
```

Scatterplots:

```
> pairs(iris[1:4])
> plot(Petal.Length~Petal.Width, iris)   # plot(y~x) is equivalent to plot(x, y)
> coplot(Petal.Length~Petal.Width | Species, iris)   # Conditioning plot
```

Count data in contingency tables:

```
> x=HairEyeColor[, , 2]
> addmargins(x)      # 2-way contingency table
> barplot(x, beside=T, legend=T)
> dotchart(x)
> dotchart(prop.table(x)*100)
> mosaicplot(x)
```

Cell means[12]:

```
x=with(warpbreaks, tapply(breaks, list(wool, tension), mean))   # Cell means
> barplot(x, beside=T, legend=T)
> with(warpbreaks, interaction.plot(wool, tension, breaks))
> with(warpbreaks, interaction.plot(tension, wool, breaks))
```

---

[12] See also function plotmeans in package gplots for cell means with error bars, and function intxplot in package HH for an interaction plot with error bars.

Low Level Graphics

Low level graphics	
points	Plot points at given coordinates
lines	Draw lines between given coordinates
text	Draw text at given coordinates
mtext	Draw text in the margins of a plot
abline	Draw a line of given intercept and slope, or a horizontal and/or vertical line
axis	Add an axis
arrows	Draw arrows
segments	Draw line segments
rect	Draw rectangles
polygon	Draw polygons
box	Draw a box around the plot
grid	Add a rectangular grid
legend	Add a legend (a key)
title	Add labels

For example:

```
> y=rnorm(100)
> x=jitter(y,amount=2)
> plot(y~x)                              # Begin a high-level plot
> abline(h=mean(y),v=mean(x),col="grey")   # Annotate with low-level functions
> abline(lm(y~x),col="grey",lty=2)
> arrows(mean(x)+1,mean(y) − 1,mean(x)+.1,mean(y) − .1,col="blue")
> text(mean(x)+1.2,mean(y)−1.1,"Means intersect",col="blue")
```

Graphics Parameters

Graphics parameters	
main	Title of the plot
ylab, xlab	Labels for the y-axis and x-axis
ylim, xlim	Limits for the y-axis and x-axis
type	Plot type (points, lines, both, ...),
pch	Plot character (circles, dots, triangles, symbols, ...)
cex	Character expansion (size of plot characters)
lty	Line type (solid, dots, dashes, ...)
lwd	Line width
col	Colour of plot characters
	...and many others, see: help(par)

Graphics parameters enable control of the size and shape of the plotting region, the layout and calibration of axes, and the appearance, colour, and size of points, lines, text, and other symbols that appear in graphs. The graphics parameters have default values that can be set globally.[13]

Most of the parameters can be set locally by passing arguments to graphics functions. The size, shape, and colour can be set using arguments cex ("character expansion"), pch ("plot character"), and col ("colour"). These parameters take vector values which are recycled to match the number of points plotted in order to control each plotted point individually. The first element in the vector controls the first plotted point, the second controls the second point, and so on.

Title and axis labels
The text of titles and labels can include typeset mathematical symbols.[14] Labels can be suppressed by passing the empty string xlab="", ylab="", and drawn subsequently using title.

```
> plot(1:10, main="My plot", ylab="y axis", xlab="x axis")
> plot(1:10, ylab="", xlab="")                              # Suppress axis labels
> title(main="My plot", ylab="y axis", xlab="x axis")   # Add title and labels
```

Axis calibration
Axes are calculated from the range of the data being plotted. The limits can be overridden using arguments ylim and xlim. Logarithmic scales are set using log="y" and log="x", or log="xy" for both axes. The axes and the box around the plot can be suppressed using arguments frame=FALSE or axes=FALSE. Custom axes can be drawn on any of the four sides using function axis.

```
> plot(1:10, ylim=c(-10, 10), xlim=c(-10, 10))
> plot(1:10, ylim=c(10, -10), xlim=c(-10, 10))   # Reverse scale of y-axis
> plot(1:10, log="y", ylab="log(y)")              # Logarithmic y-axis
> plot(1:10, frame=FALSE)                         # Axes but no box
> plot(1:10, axes=FALSE)                          # No axes or box
> axis(side=1, at=1:10, LETTERS[1:10])            # Draw a custom x-axis
> box()                                           # Add a box around the plot
> grid()                                          # Add a grid
```

---

[13] See: help(par) for a list of the graphics parameters and information about how to set parameter values. Call function par() without arguments for a list of the default values. Most of the parameters can be set locally by passing arguments to graphics functions. For example the colour, size, and shape of plotted characters, the style of plotted lines, and so forth. A few can only be set globally by a call to par. For example the parameters that control the size of the plot region and margins. A few can only be set locally as they do not have global defaults. These include the title and axis labels which inherit their values from the names of the variables being plotted.

[14] See: help(plotmath) and help(expression).

Plot type
The plot, points, and lines functions have a type argument for broadly controlling the type of plot that is drawn. Plot types are specified by letters.[15]

```
> plot(1:10, type="l")   # Lines
> plot(1:10, type="b")   # Both points and lines
> plot(1:10, type="n")   # No plot (establish axes for subsequent annotation)
```

Line types
Line types (dots, dashes, and so forth) are specified by numbers or strings passed to
the lty argument.[16]

```
> plot(0:6, type="n", ylab="lty")
> segments(1, 0:6, 7, 0:6, lty=0:6)   # The range of provided line types
> plot(1:10, lty=2)                   # Dashed lines
```

Plot characters
The shapes of plotted points (circles, dots, and so forth) are specified by numbers
passed to the pch argument.[17] Plot characters may also be single literal characters.
Use text or mtext to plot strings.

```
> plot(1:25, pch=1:25, cex=1.5, bg="pink")   # The range of provided shapes
> plot(1:26, pch=LETTERS[1:26])              # Literal characters
> text(c(5, 20), c(20, 5), labels=c("Hello", "Hello\nWorld"))   # Strings
```

Character size
The size can be changed using a character expansion factor passed to the cex
argument.

```
> plot(1:20, cex=1:20)   # Scaling up the character size
```

Colours
The colour of plotted points is specified by numbers,[18] names,[19] or RGB values[20]
passed to the col argument. Functions are provided to calculate vectors of colour
values for colour gradations or ramps.[21]

---

[15] See: help(plot) for the list of types and the letters used to specify them.
[16] See lty "and Line Type Specification" in help(par).
[17] See: help(points) for a description of pch values.
[18] See palette() for the colour names that are indexed when col is given a numeric vector.
[19] See colours() for the available colour names.
[20] See help(rgb) for RGB (Red,Green,Blue) colour values.
[21] See: help(gray), help(rainbow), help(colorRamp), and functions in package help(RColorBrewer).

```
> plot(1:20, col=1:20, pch=16)   # The range of colours in the default palette
> plot(1:20, pch=16, col=c("red", "green", "blue"))      # Colour names (recycled)
> plot(1:20, pch=16, col=gray(0:20/20))              # Gray ramp
> plot(1:20, pch=16, col=colorRampPalette(c("blue", "yellow"))(20))   # Colour ramp
```

Grouping Points by Colour or Shape

Groups of points on a scatter plot can be plotted in their own colours and shapes.
One way is to plot each group separately, beginning with plot and using points
to add subsequent groups. A better way, because the scale is established for all
the groups, is to index colours and shapes with a grouping factor. For example
to scatter plot two of the iris measures, indicating the three species of iris on
the plot:

```
> my.colours=c("red", "green3", "blue")
> my.shapes=16:18
> plot(Sepal.Length~Petal.Length, data=iris,  pch=my.shapes[iris$Species],
+                                              col=my.colours[iris$Species])
```

Adding a Legend

Add a legend using the legend function. This can be positioned by passing
arguments for the plot coordinates of its top-left corner, or by using keywords
such as "topleft" and "bottomright" and the inset argument. Alternatively
the legend can be positioned interactively using the locator function. Use left-
click to locate the legend's top-left corner, then right-click and choose Stop.

```
> my.text=levels(iris$Species)
> legend("bottomright", inset=.05, legend=my.text, pch=my.shapes, col=my.colours)
> legend(locator(), inset=.05, legend=my.text, pch=my.shapes, col=my.colours)
```

Identifying Plotted Points Interactively

Points on a scatterplot can be identified using the identify function, which
returns the row names of identified points. To use this, left-click one or more
points, then right-click and choose Stop. (Note: this function uses x,y coordinates
and does not have a formula interface).

```
> identify(iris$Petal.Length, iris$Sepal.Length)
```

3.2.2 Lattice Graphics

The lattice[22] package provides graphics functions based on the idea of a multi-panel conditioning plot.

Lattice plots are not built up by successive graphics functions; the whole plot must be defined with a single function call. Lattice functions return an object. This enables the whole graph to be saved and plotted later using generic print or plot.

Lattice graphics	
xyplot	Multi-panel conditioning scatterplot
barchart	Bar plot
dotplot	Dot plot
splom	Scatterplot matrix
bwplot	Box-and-whisker plot
histogram	Histogram
densityplot	Smoothed histogram

Lattice functions take formula and data arguments. The formula may include a grouping variable to organise the multi-panel layout, as in: y ~ x | g, which can be read as "plot y on x grouped by g". Each group is plotted in a separate panel. The grouping variable g is a factor, or a vector which may be cut into shingles (overlapping ranges) using function equal.count. For example:

```
> library(lattice)
> xyplot(Sepal.Length~Petal.Length, data=iris)
> xyplot(Sepal.Length~Petal.Length | Species, data=iris)
> # Setting the colour and shape of the plot characters:
> xyplot(Sepal.Length~Petal.Length | Species, data=iris, col="black", pch=16)
```

The optional groups argument controls how information is superposed within panels. (This argument is ignored by bwplot and histogram where it makes no sense to superpose graphics).

```
> xyplot(Sepal.Length~Petal.Length, groups=Species, data=iris)
> # Setting the colour and shape of superposed plot characters:
> cols=c("red", "green3", "blue")
> shps=16:18
> xyplot(Sepal.Length~Petal.Length, groups=Species, data=iris, col=cols, pch=shps)
```

The type of plot within each panel is controlled either by the type argument or, for extra control, by the panel argument. The type argument selects from a

---

[22] Lattice is an implementation of S-language trellis graphics. The name "trellis" comes from the notion that a multi-panel conditioning plot looks somewhat like a garden trellis.

limited range of plot styles specified by letters,[23] for example "p" for points, and "r" for a regression line:

```
> xyplot(Sepal.Length~Petal.Length | Species, data=iris, type=c('p', 'r'))
> xyplot(Sepal.Length~Petal.Length, groups=Species, data=iris, type=c('p', 'r'))
```

For example a trellis plot of growth-curve data:

```
> data(sleepstudy, package="lme4")
> xyplot(Reaction~Days | Subject, data=sleepstudy, type='b')
> xyplot(Reaction~Days | Subject, data=sleepstudy, type=c('p', 'r'))
```

The panel argument allows you to pass a panel function to specify exactly how to plot each panel. (This argument is ignored by bwplot, densityplot, and barchart, where it makes no sense to choose between plot types such as points or lines). Many panel functions are provided for different kinds of plots.[24] Alternatively the panel function may be custom defined as a combination of available panel functions, each with individually specified arguments. For example:

```
> xyplot(Reaction~Days | Subject, data=sleepstudy,
+   panel=function(x, y) {
+     panel.grid()
+     panel.xyplot(x, y, col="black", pch=20)
+     panel.lmline(x, y, col="blue")})
```

Panels can be annotated with points, lines, text, arrows, and so forth using low-level functions.[25]

3.2.3 Multiple Plot Layout

Base Graphics

Each time a high-level graphics function is called the new plot replaces any previous plot. Several high-level functions allow an argument add=TRUE to prevent this, so that successive high-level plots can be superposed. Successive high-level plots on a graphics device can also be layed out in a grid of panels.

---

[23] See: help(panel.xyplot) for the list of types and the letters used to specify them.
[24] See: apropos("^panel").
[25] See: help(panel.points).

Multiple plot layout	
par(mfrow), par(mfcol)	Set a grid layout of fixed size
layout	Set a grid layout of specified sizes
split.screen	Split a graphics device into multiple screens

The par options mfrow or mfcol take a vector of two elements specifying the number of rows and columns for the grid, and subsequent plots are drawn by columns mfcol or by rows mfrow. The layout function specifies the grid using a matrix of integers in which each integer refers to the number of the plot in succession. This allows you to merge grid panels by using the same plot number in adjacent positions in the matrix. The layout function also has widths and heights arguments to specify the absolute size of each panel.

```
> par(mfrow=c(2,2))         # 2 x 2layout
> sapply(iris[1:4],hist)     # Plot four histograms (iris data)
> layout(matrix(1:4,nrow=2,byrow=T))   # ... same thing using layout
> sapply(iris[1:4],hist)
> layout(matrix(c(1,1,2,3),nrow=2,byrow=T))   # Merging panels
> sapply(iris[1:3],hist)  # ... plot three histograms
> layout(matrix(1),widths=1cm(10),heights=1cm(10))   # Specify absolute size
> hist(iris[[1]],main="Plot size is 10cm x 10cm")
```

The split.screen function enables panels within a single device to be treated as separate devices, (called "screens"). Subsequent plots can be addressed to any screen, and high-level plots can be superposed on the same screen.

```
> y=1:1000; x=rexp(1000)
> split.screen(c(1,1))          # 1 x 1 layout
> hist(x,col="tan",axes=F)      # Draw a plot
> screen(1,new=FALSE)           # Make screen 1 active without erasing
> plot(x,y,col="seagreen")      # Overplot
> close.screen(all=TRUE)        # Exit split-screen mode
```

Lattice Graphics

Multiple plot layouts in lattice graphics are controlled by the print method's split argument.[26] For example:

---

[26] See: help(print.trellis).

```
> p1=xyplot(Petal.Length~Petal.Width | Species, iris, type=c('p', 'r'))
> p2=xyplot(Sepal.Length~Sepal.Width | Species, iris, type=c('p', 'r'))
> print(p1, split=c(1, 1,  2, 1), more=T)   # Plot at (1, 1) within 2x1 grid
> print(p2, split=c(2, 1,  2, 1))           # Plot at (2, 1) within 2x1 grid
```

3.2.4 Saving Graphics

Graphics functions produce displays by sending instructions to a "graphics device". The default device is the monitor screen, but other graphics devices[27] include PDF files and image files in various formats including jpeg and bmp. Each device has "driver" software that translates the device-independent plotting instructions sent by the graphics function into device-specific plotting instructions.

Each device has a function to "open" it, (making its driver software available for use). Several devices can be open at any time, but only one can be "active"[28] in the sense that it receives all plotting instructions. Normally, (unless other devices are already open), a window on the monitor screen is opened whenever you use a graphics command or the par function. To plot instead to a PDF file in the current working folder:

```
> pdf(file="foo.pdf")   # Open the PDF device to write to a named file
> plot(x)               # One or more plotting functions come here
> dev.off()             # Flush output to the graphics device and close it
```

Unless you particularly want a PDF or image file, the simplest way to save a graph under Windows is to display the graph on the monitor, right-click on it, and choose one of the copy or save options. For example Copy as metafile copies the graph to the Windows clipboard from where it can be pasted directly into an application such as Word or PowerPoint.

---

[27] See: help(Devices) for a list of the available graphics devices.
[28] See: help(dev.cur).

Chapter 4
Hypothesis Tests

Abstract Probability distributions and hypothesis testing in R.

Keywords Inference · Probability · Parametric tests · Nonparametric tests

4.1 Probability Distributions

R provides functions that serve the purpose of built-in probability tables.

Normal probability distribution	
rnorm	Random sample from a normal distribution
dnorm	Probability density function
qnorm	Quantile: critical value of the cumulative distribution to limit a given area
pnorm	Probability: area under the cumulative distribution limited by a given quantile

The corresponding functions for other distributions (with names respectively prefixed by r, d q, and p) include: t, f, binom, pois, chisq, exp, weibull, geom, hyper, logis, beta, gamma.

The quantile and probability functions (with names prefixed q and p) refer to an interval on the left side of the distribution. Use argument lower.tail=FALSE to refer to the interval on the right side.

```
> qnorm(0.025, lower.tail=F)     # Critical value q for P[z > q]=0.025
> pnorm(1.96, lower.tail=F) * 2   # P[z <= -1.96 or z > 1.96](2-tailed)
```

The empirical distribution-free equivalent to the q and p functions are quantile and ecdf (empirical cumulative distribution function). The ecdf function returns a function, which in turn is used to calculate the probability to the left side

M. Allerhand, *A Tiny Handbook of R*, SpringerBriefs in Statistics, 59
DOI: 10.1007/978-3-642-17980-8_4, © Springer-Verlag Berlin Heidelberg 2011

of a given quantile. Subtract the probability from 1 to obtain the probability
on the right side.

```
> x = rnorm(10000)              # If the sample is normal then...
> quantile(x, probs=0.975)      # ..is like: qnorm(0.025, lower.tail=F)
> psamp = ecdf(x)               # (note ecdf returns a function)
> (1 − psamp(1.96)) ∗ 2         # ..is like: pnorm(1.96, lower.tail=F) ∗ 2
```

4.2 Hypothesis Tests

The hypothesis tests provided in the base installation include[1]:

Hypothesis tests	
t.test	one and two-sample t tests
wilcox.test	one and two sample Wilcoxon tests
var.test	one and two sample F-tests of variance
cor.test	Correlation coefficient and p-value (Pearson's, Spearman's, or Kendall's)
binom.test	Sign test of a binomial sample
prop.test	Binomial test for comparing two proportions
chisq.test	Chi-squared test for count data
fisher.test	Fisher's exact test for count data
friedman.test	Friedman's rank sum test
kruskal.test	Kruskal–Wallis rank sum test
ks.test	1 or 2-sample Kolmogorov–Smirnov tests

4.2.1 How to Run a t test

Functions t.test and wilcox.test are respectively the parametric and nonparametric hypothesis tests for a mean (one sample) or a mean difference (two
samples).

The one-sample test is of the null that the population of values from which a
sample is drawn has mean 0, (or some particular mean value passed as the
argument mu). To run a one-sample test pass just one numeric vector, (so argument
y remains NULL). For example:

```
> x = rnorm(20, mean=10)   # Random sample
> t.test(x)                # H1: mean(x) != 0
> t.test(x, mu=10)         # H1: mean(x) != 10
```

---

[1] See also: apropos("\\.test$")

The two-sample test is of the null that the difference between the two sample means is 0, (so that the two samples might be drawn from the same population). A value may be passed to argument mu to test a particular difference in means.

The two-sample test can be run in two ways,[2] for data that are either in wide or in long format. The traditional (x,y) interface is the more appropriate for wide format data. The formula (y ~ g) interface is the more appropriate for long format data. The variable on the left side of the formula (y) is a numeric vector that contains both samples, and the variable on the right side (g) is a 2-level grouping factor to indicate which sample each element of y belongs to.

For example the provided data set sleep contains Student's sleep data in long format:

```
> sleep                         # Long format (variable and grouping factor)
> unstack(sleep, extra~group)   # Wide format (two vectors)
```

A t.test using the formula interface:

```
> t.test(extra~group,  data=sleep,  paired=TRUE)
```

The paired argument specifies whether the two samples are to be treated as independent and unpaired, (the default), or as related and paired,[3] (using: paired=TRUE), in which case the two groups must be the same size.

The function returns an object from which information can be extracted by name,[4] for example:

```
> x=t.test(extra~group, data=sleep, paired=TRUE)
> names(x)        # The names of the object's components
> x$statistic   # The t statistic
> x$parameter   # The degrees-of-freedom
> x$p.value     # The p-value
```

The unpaired t.test applies a correction by default for unequal variances which results in fractional degrees-of-freedom. For whole-numbered degrees-of-freedom, assuming variances are equal, use var.equal=TRUE:

```
> t.test(extra~group, data=sleep)                  # Un-paired
> t.test(extra~group, data=sleep, var.equal=TRUE)  # Equal variance assumed
```

Functions for hypothesis tests have an alternative argument, (which can be abbreviated to alt), to control whether the p-values are to be 2-tailed, (the default), or 1-tailed with a given alternative hypothesis, (using: alt="less" or

---

[2] See the "Usage" section of help(t.test) and help(wilcox.test).

[3] The unpaired wilcox.test is the Wilcoxon rank sum or Mann-Whitney test. The paired test is Wilcoxon's signed ranks test.

[4] See the "Value" section in help(t.test).

alt="greater"). The direction of the 1-tailed prediction depends upon the positional order of the arguments or, (for the formula interface), the order of the factor levels.

```
> # Using the x, y interface:
> t.test(x, y, alt="two.sided")         # H1: mean(x) != mean(y) (default)
> t.test(x, y, alt="less")              #H1: mean(x) < mean(y)
> t.test(x, y, alt="greater")           # H1: mean(x) > mean(y)
> # Using the formula interface:
> t.test(y~g, data=d, alt="two.sided")  # H1: level1 mean != level2 mean
> t.test(y~g, data=d, alt="less")       # H1: level1 mean < level2 mean
> t.test(y~g, data=d, alt="greater")    # H1: level1 mean > level2 mean
```

The functions treat missing values by silently omitting cases with NA. This default behaviour can be changed by passing a function to handle missing values as the na.action argument.

Chapter 5
Linear Models

Abstract Fitting general linear models in R.

Keywords Multiple regression · Analysis of variance

5.1 Model Formulas

Linear modelling functions such as lm have a model formula as their mandatory first argument. The model formula, together with the contrast coding system, is the interface to the model-fitting function that enables you programmatically to specify a wide range of models, including multiple regression models, ANOVA and ANCOVA models, and their multivariate counterparts. The formula is a symbolic description[1] of the model, and represents the additive effects in algebraic form in terms of the computational objects that store the data.

The general form is: $y \sim$ model, where y is the dependent or response variable, and the model is specified on the right side of the tilde as a linear predictor consisting of a series of terms separated by + signs. For example:

```
> lm(y ~ x1 + x2, data)   # Regress y onto x1 and x2
```

Terms are included in a formula using the + sign, or excluded using a − sign. These operators[2] are not arithmetic addition and subtraction in this context.

---

[1] Wilkinson, G. N. and Rogers, C. E. (1973) Symbolic descriptions of factorial models for analysis of variance. Applied Statistics, 22, 392–9.
[2] See: help(formula).

For example a formula containing x1+x1 does not mean that the variable x1 is to be added to itself. Here the second x1 is redundant and is not used. If necessary arithmetic operations can be embedded in a formula using the function I temporarily to escape the formula interpretation of operators. For example I(x1+x2) includes a single term derived from two variables as the value of the arithmetic expression. Similarly to derive a term as a squared variable use I(x^2). Functions that transform variables may appear in a formula, such as log(x) and sqrt(x).

The variables that appear in model terms are numeric vectors[3] or factors. Factors are internally replaced by dummy numeric variables.

A product term (an interaction) is denoted using the : operator. For example x1:x2 denotes a single term that is the product of two variables. This is equivalent to I(x1*x2) when the variables are both numeric. The : operator is necessary if either variable is a factor, when arithmetic is not directly valid and a product must be defined in a special way in terms of the dummy variables.

For example if x is numeric and a is a 3-level factor the product x:a consists of two terms: x:a2 + x:a3, where a1 and a2 are two dummy numeric variables for factor a. If b is a 2-level factor the product a:b consists of two terms: a2:b2 + a3:b2, all dummy numeric variables.

A syntactic convenience using the * operator is provided to simplify formulation of the typical 2-way factorial design that includes all marginal terms. For example a*b is equivalent to a+b+a:b. Further, a*b*c is equivalent to a+b+c+a:b+a:c+b:c+a:b:c.

The ^2 operator denotes main effects and product terms up to second-order. For example (a+b+c)^2 is equivalent to a+b+c+a:b+a:c+b:c. Similarly ^3 denotes main effects and product terms up to third-order.

The formula syntax is algebraically distributive. For example (a+b)*c is equivalent to a*c+b*c, which in turn is equivalent to a+b+c+a:c+b:c. Terms can be dropped using the − operator. For example (a+b)*c−b:c is equivalent to a+b+c+a:c.

The intercept term is represented by the number 1. An intercept term is included by default and does not need to appear in a formula, unless it is to specify an intercept only. For example y ∼ x is equivalent to y ∼ 1+x since the intercept is assumed by default. The model y ∼ 1 is the unconditional intercept-only (null) model. To force the intercept to be 0 in the model use either 0 or −1. For example: y ∼ 0+x or y ∼ x−1.

---

[3] Logical vectors are treated numerically, TRUE=>1, FALSE=>0. Character vectors are internally converted to factors.

Some examples[4] of model formulas:

Model	Formula	
$y = \beta_0 + \beta_1 x + e$	y ~ x	Simple regression
$y = \beta_0 + \beta_1 x_1 + \beta_2 x_2 + e$	y ~ x1+x2	Multiple regression
$y = \beta_0 + e$	y ~ 1	Intercept only (null) model
$y = \beta_1 x + e$	y ~ 0+x	Slope only
$y = \beta_0 + \beta_1 x_1 + \beta_2 x_2 + \beta_3 x_1 x_2 + e$	y ~ x1*x2	Main effects and products
	y ~ x1+x2+x1:x2	
$y = \beta_0 + \beta_1 x + \beta_2 x^2 + e$	y ~ x+I(x^2)	Quadratic term
$ln(y) = \beta_0 + \beta_1 x_1 + \beta_2 x_2 + e$	log(y) ~ x1+x2	Log dependent

5.1.1 Formula and Data Frame

Functions that take a formula argument also take an optional argument named data for passing a data frame to the function. The function looks first in the data frame for the variables referred to in the model formula, and then looks outside for variables not found or if the data frame is omitted.

There are two advantages to passing a data frame to the function. Firstly it is a convenient way to control the data supplied to the function. For example to drop cases indexed by i from a data frame dat the argument would be: data=dat [-i,]. Secondly it provides variable names (column names) to the function, and this enables a syntactic convenience in the model formula whereby a . is used to represent all the variables found in the data frame except those already specified on the left-side of the formula as dependents. For example if the data frame contains variables named: y, x1, x2, and x3, then the shorthand model formula y~. is equivalent to the formula: y ~ x1+x2+x3. The shorthand model formula y ~ (.)^2 is equivalent to: y ~ (x1+x2+x3)^2.

This is useful for specifying a full model when the data frame contains many variables. It also facilitates dropping terms using a − sign. For example using the same data frame the formula y ~ .−x1 would be equivalent to the formula: y ~ x2+x3.

5.1.2 Updating Model Fits

The update function takes the results of a previously fitted model and updates the fit, applying a new formula that specifies changes relative to the previous model.

---

[4] For further examples see section: "Defining statistical models; formulae" in the manual "An Introduction to R" displayed by help.start().

The formula uses the same syntax with the addition that . can also represent the dependent, since the dependent can be identified in the fit that is being updated. For example a fitted model named fit is re-fitted dropping variable x1 by: update(fit, .~. − x1).

The modelling functions treat missing values by silently omitting cases with NA in the modelled variables. This default behaviour can be changed by passing a function to handle missing values as the na.action argument.

Functions for fitting linear models	
lm	General linear model
aov	Analysis of variance (lm with syntax for repeated-measures)
glm	Generalized linear model
update	Update and re-fit a general or generalized linear model
summary.lm	Regression coefficients and t-tests (standard "last-term-in" regression)
summary.aov	Sums of squares and F-tests (sequential type-I anova table)
Anova(car)	Sums of squares (optionally types II or III)
add1, drop1	Tests of single-term additions or deletions
step	Searching models stepwise to minimize AIC
anova.lm	Analysis of variance of lm fit
anova.glm	Analysis of deviance of glm fit
lmer(lme4)	Linear Mixed-effects models

5.2 General Linear Models

The provided swiss data set[5] contains numeric measures relating to fertility in 47 provinces of Switzerland.

```
> dim(swiss)
> sapply(swiss, class)
```

Exploring the variables:

```
> boxplot(swiss)
> pairs(swiss, panel=panel.smooth)
> cor(swiss)
> round(cor(swiss)^2 * 100, 1)   # Percentage shared variance
```

Fit a regression model by ordinary least squares using the lm (linear model) function. Printing the object returned by lm displays the estimated regression coefficients.

---

[5] See: help(swiss).

```
> lm(Fertility~., swiss)                    # Regression coefficients
> lm(Fertility~., data.frame(scale(swiss)))  # Standardized "beta" coefficients
```

5.2.1 Regression Diagnostics

The object returned by lm contains other information including the model fitted values and the residuals. When plotted it displays a series of diagnostic plots[6]:

```
> fit = lm(Fertility~., swiss)
> names(fit)          # Names of the components of the returned object
> fit$fitted          # Fitted values
> fit$resid           # Residuals
> par(mfrow=c(2, 2))  # Four diagnostic plots...
> plot(fit)
```

5.2.2 Testing the Regression Coefficients

The lm object's summary method,[7] summary.lm, calculates standard errors and t tests for each coefficient and displays overall goodness-of-fit information. Each model term is assessed as if it were the last to be entered in the model. That is, each term is assessed taking account of all the other terms in the model.

```
> summary.lm(fit)   # Coefficients, t tests, and goodness-of-fit
> confint(fit)      # 95% CI around estimates
```

---

[6] For normality see help(qqnorm) and transformations (Tukey's "ladder of powers"). For unequal variances see help(levene.test, package=car) and the weights argument for lm, for example: weights=1/predict(fit). For outlier diagnostics see also: help(influence.measures), help(cooks.distance), help(dffits), and help(dfbetas).

[7] R has several "generic" functions. Generic functions select more specialized functions, called "methods", depending upon the class of object they are passed as argument. The aim is to provide a unified point of call to implement the generic meaning of the function for different kinds of data object. See help(UseMethod) and help(Methods). By convention a method's name is made up of the generic function name followed by the class. For example the summary method for lm objects, (objects returned by the linear model function lm), is called summary.lm. Similarly the summary method for aov objects, (returned by the analysis of variance function aov), is called summary.aov. The help page for a generic function describes just the generic behaviour of the function. Usually you'll want the help page for the particular method which describes the arguments and the object returned. For example help(summary) describes generic behaviour, but help(summary.lm) describes the function that is selected when an lm object is passed to summary.

5.2.3 Prediction

The predict.lm function takes a fitted lm object and returns the model predicted outcome for given data. For example to predict the outcome for a particular province if the percentage of Education in the province is increased to 60%:

```
> predict.lm(fit, newdata=transform(swiss[45, ], Education=60))
```

5.2.4 Stepwise Regression

Terms can be entered in blocks using separate lm fits, and the blocks tested sequentially using the anova.lm model comparison function:

```
> fit1 = lm(Fertility ~ Education, swiss)
> fit2 = update(fit1, . ~ . + Examination, swiss)
> fit3 = update(fit2, . ~ . + Agriculture, swiss)
> fit4 = update(fit3, . ~ . + (Catholic + Infant.Mortality), swiss)
> anova(fit1, fit2, fit3, fit4)
```

Model development or simplification is aided by a group of functions: add1, drop1, step, and anova.lm. Functions add1 and drop1 carry out 1df tests to assess the effect of single-term addition or deletion on the amount of variation explained. The drop1 function compares the full model with the model with one term deleted for each term in the model.[8] A subset of terms can be specified for deletion by giving a formula to the scope argument. The add1 function tests single-term additions, taking the terms for addition from a formula given as the scope argument. The step function attempts to automate model simplification, using add1 and drop1 repeatedly to search a set of models with the aim of finding the model with the lowest AIC.[9] The anova function can carry out 1df or multiple df model comparison tests. Multiple df tests can be used to assess the benefit of adding/deleting sets of terms, for example sets of highly correlated multi-collinear variables.

```
> fit = lm(Fertility ~ ., swiss)                      # Full model
> fit1 = update(fit, . ~ . − Examination)             # ...less one term
> fit2 = update(fit, . ~ . − (Examination+Agriculture)) # ...less two terms
> anova(fit1, fit)                                     # 1df test (one deletion)
> anova(fit2, fit)                                     # Multiple df test (two deletions)
> drop1(fit, test="F")                                 # All single-term deletions
> step(fit)                                            # Stepwise model selection
```

---

[8] Since drop1 tests each term as if it were the "last-term-in", it is the same as type-III anova.
[9] See also functions logLik and AIC.

5.2.5 Extracting Information from the Fit Object

The objects returned by functions such as lm and summary.lm contain multiple values encapsulated within a single object that has a list structure. The components of the list have names and can be extracted from the list by name:

```
> names(fit)                   # See ?lm
> names(summary(fit))          # See ?summary.lm
> fit$coef                     # Estimated coefficients
> fit$resid                    # Residuals
> fit$fitted                   # Fitted values
> summary(fit)$fstatistic      # Overall F-statistic
> summary(fit)$r.squared       # Multiple R-squared
```

Information extracted from the fit object can be used to calculate effect sizes. For example Cohen's f^2 effect size for multiple regression:

```
> r2 = summary(fit)$r.squared   # Multiple R-squared
> r2 * 100                      # Percentage variation explained by the model
> r2/(1-r2)                     # Cohens f2 effect size for regression
```

5.2.6 Residualizing

Residuals can be extracted from the fit object, to residualize variables and calculate shared variance and semi-partial correlations. For example the following
calculates the proportion of the variance of Agriculture that is shared (overlaps)
with the other predictors, and the proportion that is its unique contribution to the
variation in Fertility. The semi-partial correlation is obtained first by residu-
alizing (partialling-out) the other predictors from Agriculture, and with what
remains calculating the shared variance with Fertility:

```
> d = swiss[-1]   # Data frame with just the predictors
> summary(lm(Agriculture~., d))$r.squared              # Shared
> cor(swiss$Fertility, lm(Agriculture~., d)$resid)^2   # Unique
```

Calculations can be wrapped into functions and mapped (applied) to multiple
objects. As an illustration, the following calculates and plots the shared and unique
variances of each of the predictors:

```
> d = swiss[−1]
> fits = sapply(1:ncol(d), function(i) lm(d[[i]] ~ ., d[−i]), simplify=F)
> unique = sapply(fits, function(fit) cor(swiss$Fertility, fit$resid)^2)
> shared = sapply(fits, function(fit) summary(fit)$r.squared)
> x = rbind(unique, shared)
> colnames(x) = names(swiss)[−1]
> dotchart(x, xlim=0:1, main="Variance proportions")
> abline(v=0.9, lty=3, col="grey")
> 1-shared        # Tolerances
> 1/(1-shared)    # VIF (variance inflation factors)
```

5.3 ANOVA

An experimental design organises the observations into "cells". Each cell contains
a group of observations in one experimental condition. Grouping factors are used
to indicate which cell each observation belongs to.

For example the provided warpbreaks data set contains observations of the
number of breaks in yarn or thread during weaving. This is assumed to depend
upon the type of wool and the tension of the thread, and so the design of the
experiment has observations grouped by two factors: wool (two types of wool:
A or B), and tension (three levels of tension: L, M, H)[10]:

```
> warpbreaks                                        # Long format
> unstack(warpbreaks, breaks ~ wool:tension)        # Wide format
```

The design is a 2-way layout of 2x3=6 cells. The table function cross-
tabulates factors to count the replications in each cell of the design. The factors
are "fully crossed", (there are no empty cells), and the design is "balanced" (there
are equal numbers of replications in each cell).

```
> replications(~ wool:tension, warpbreaks)     # Replications per cell
> with(warpbreaks, table(wool, tension))       # Contingency table
```

The distribution of observations within cells can be explored numerically[11] and
graphically. For example it might be helpful to add a dot plot to a box-and-whisker
plot (using function stripchart) if the sample is not too large:

---

[10] A data frame of factors may be constructed to suit the design using functions such as gl, rep,
and expand.grid. For example: expand.grid(wool=gl(2,1, 18), tension=gl(3,1)).
[11] See also function levene.test in package car to test homogeneity of variance.

```
> with(warpbreaks, tapply(breaks, list(wool, tension), var))   # Cell variances
> boxplot(breaks~wool+tension, warpbreaks)
> stripchart(breaks~wool+tension, warpbreaks, vertical=TRUE,
+               method="jitter", pch=1, add=TRUE)
```

The pattern of cell means can be explored numerically and graphically. The tapply function can be used to calculate a table of cell means, and addmargins used to add marginal means to the table. The interaction.plot function displays a profile plot of the pattern of cell means[12]:

```
> tab = with(warpbreaks, tapply(breaks, list(wool, tension), mean))   # Cell means
> tab = addmargins(tab, FUN=mean, quiet=TRUE)   # Add marginal means to the table
> names(dimnames(tab))=c("Wool", "Tension")      # Add dimnames names
> round(tab, 2)                                   # Print the table rounded to 2dp
> with(warpbreaks, interaction.plot(tension, wool, breaks, type='b', pch=16:17))
```

5.3.1 ANOVA Tables

Function aov and its summary method summary.aov are used to calculate sums-of-squares and carry out F tests.[13]

One-Way ANOVA

The summary.aov function takes the object returned by aov, (or by lm), and displays a traditional ANOVA table of sums-of-squares, mean squares, and

---

[12] Swap the order of the arguments to transpose the table and the plot. If the data contain NAs these can be omitted from the calculation of cell means by passing na.rm=TRUE as an argument to mean via tapply. See the section: "Passing arguments to the mapped function". The interaction.plot function does not have an argument to control NA directly, but this can be done by via an anonymous mean function. See the examples in: help(interaction.plot). See also function plotmeans in package gplots for cell means with error bars, and function intxplot in package HH for an interaction plot with error bars.

[13] Function aov is essentially an ordinary least squares parameter estimator the same as function lm. The main difference is that the object returned is class aov, so that generic print and summary, respectively, select methods that display sums-of-squares, (rather than regression coefficients), and an ANOVA table of mean squares and F tests, (rather than a table of regression coefficients and t tests). See: help(aov) and help(summary.aov). The formula argument for aov also allows terms to be given within a function named Error to specify nested structures of residual errors, for repeated measures and split-plot designs. For further details see the section "Analysis of variance and model comparison" in the manual "An Introduction to R" which is displayed by the function help.start().

"omnibus" F tests. The F test is of the null that there is no difference between any of the cell means:

```
> fit = aov(breaks~ tension, warpbreaks)
> summary.aov(fit)   # Or use generic summary
```

Two-Way Factorial ANOVA

The summary.aov function calculates a "sequential" ANOVA table using "Type-I" sums-of-squares. An equivalent table calculated using "Type-II" or "Type-III" sums-of-squares can be displayed using function Anova[14]:

```
> fit = aov(breaks~ wool+tension, warpbreaks)   # Main effects only
> summary.aov(fit)
> fit = aov(breaks~ wool*tension, warpbreaks)   # With interaction
> summary.aov(fit)              # Type I SS
> car::Anova(fit, type="II")    # Type II SS
> car::Anova(fit, type="III")   # Type III SS
```

These three methods of calculating sums-of-squares have identical results if the design is balanced and the model includes no interaction terms.[15]

If the design is balanced (if the cells contain equal numbers of observations) the main effects are orthogonal and independent of each other. In that case the sums-of-squares of individual effects are additive components of the total sum-of-squares, so the variance explained by each effect can be expressed as a proportion of the total variance. If the design is unbalanced the terms will be correlated. In that case the sums-of-squares are not additive, and are different depending upon the method used to calculate them. In a sequential (Type-I) ANOVA table the sums-of-squares of the main effects depend upon the order in which they appear in the model. However the order can be manipulated to explore the shared variance between terms. In a Types-II or III table the sums-of-squares of main effects do not depend upon term order, but neither do they contain any information about shared variance.

---

[14] Function Anova, (names are case-sensitive so the upper-case A is important), is provided in package car. The :: operator can be used to access a function within a library without having to load the whole library. See help("::").

[15] Type I: Terms of the same degree, (such as all the main effect terms, or all the second-order product terms), are assessed sequentially in the order that they appear in the model. Higher-order terms are always assessed after lower-order terms. For example interactions are always assessed after their marginal main effects.

Type II: Terms of the same degree are assessed after accounting for all other terms of the same degree, as if each were the last term of that degree in the model. Higher-order terms are assessed after lower-order terms.

Type III: Each term is assessed after accounting for all other terms in the model, irrespective of degree.

If the model includes an interaction the sums-of-squares depend upon the method used to calculate them. Default R functions such as summary.aov respect the "principle of marginality" which requires that interactions are always assessed after accounting for their marginal main effects. If the interaction is significant it is questionable whether its marginal main effects can meaningfully be interpreted. In this example the interaction is weakly significant and hardly dominates its marginal main effects. However the significance of the wool effect depends upon whether it is assessed before the interaction, (Type-I), or after (Type-III).

Model Comparison

The model comparison function anova.lm provides a flexible alternative to the full sequential ANOVA table displayed by summary.aov. It enables terms or blocks of terms to be assessed by comparing two or more nested model fits.

```
> fit1 = aov(breaks ~ wool, warpbreaks)
> fit2 = aov(breaks ~ wool+tension, warpbreaks)
> anova.lm(fit1, fit2)   # Or use generic anova
```

An additional advantage of anova.lm is that it is slightly easier to extract information from the object it returns than from the object returned by summary.aov.[16] For example to extract degrees-of-freedom, sums-of-squares, and mean-squares to derive some effect sizes[17]:

```
> fit = aov(breaks ~ wool*tension, warpbreaks)
> tab = anova.lm(fit)        # ANOVA table
> p = nrow(tab)              # Number of terms including the residual
> df = tab[, 1]              # Degrees-of-freedom (1st column of the table)
> SS = tab[, 2]              # Sums-of-squares (2nd column)
> MS = tab[, 3]              # Mean-squares (3rd column)
> SS/sum(SS)                 # Proportions of each SS
> sum(SS[-p])/sum(SS)        # Multiple R-squared
> SS[-p]/(SS[-p]+SS[p])      # Partial eta squared
> vars = (MS[-p] - MS[p]) * df[-p]/(sum(df)+1)  # Variances
> vars/(sum(vars)+MS[p])     # Partial omega squared
```

---

[16] The object returned by anova.lm is a single ANOVA table. The object returned by summary.aov is a list of ANOVA tables, one for each "error stratum".

[17] Partial eta squared is the effect size of each effect derived from the sums-of-squares as SS/(SS+SS.error). Partial omega squared is the estimated population effect size of each effect, derived from variances rather than sums-of-squares.

5.3.2 Comparisons

Pairwise comparisons test particular mean differences within an omnibus effect.

Post-hoc Tests

Use function `pairwise.t.test` or `TukeyHSD` for pairwise comparisons.[18]

```
> with(warpbreaks, pairwise.t.test(breaks, wool, p.adj="bonferroni"))
> with(warpbreaks, pairwise.t.test(breaks, tension, p.adj="bonferroni"))
> with(warpbreaks, pairwise.t.test(breaks, wool:tension, p.adj="bonferroni"))
> fit = aov(breaks~wool*tension, warpbreaks)
> TukeyHSD(fit)
```

Alternatively use function `glht`[19] in package `multcomp`.

```
> library(multcomp)
> summary(glht(fit, linfct=mcp(tension="Tukey")))
> confint(glht(fit, linfct=mcp(tension="Tukey")))
```

Planned Comparisons

To obtain maximum precision, avoiding the p-value adjustments used to compensate for family-wise error rate, limit the number of pairwise comparisons to a subset of planned comparisons of interest. This is done by controlling the contrast coding of dummy variables.

Factors in a model formula, (representing categorical variables), are automatically replaced by numerical dummy variables to form a regression equation. Each k-level factor is replaced internally by $k-1$ dummy variables. An interaction between a k_1-level and a k_2-level factor is replaced by $(k_1 - 1) * (k_2 - 1)$ dummy variables. For example in the `warpbreaks` data, `wool` (a 2-level factor) has one dummy variable, `tension` (a 3-level factor) has two dummy variables, and their interaction `wool:tension` has $(2-1)*(3-1)=2$ dummy variables. There are six terms (including the intercept) in this fully factorial model.

The dummy variables are given numerical values by a system of contrast coding. The numerical values given to dummy variables are designed to set up comparisons between factor levels. The values are contrived so that the resulting regression coefficients represent mean differences for pairwise comparisons.

---

[18] See `help(p.adjust)` for alternative methods of adjusting for the family-wise error rate.
[19] The `glht` function has methods for `lmer` (linear mixed-effects) fits providing a route to post-hoc tests for repeated measures designs.

The contrast coding is specified in order to bring out and test comparisons of interest.[20]

The model.matrix function displays the design matrix, showing how a model formula is expanded into terms and how factors are represented by dummy numeric variables. For example the default contrast coding:

```
> model.matrix(~ tension, warpbreaks)        # 1-way
> model.matrix(~ wool+tension, warpbreaks)   # 2-way
> model.matrix(~ wool*tension, warpbreaks)   # 2-way with interaction
```

Dummy variables for interaction terms are designed to respect the principle of marginality.[21] If a marginal term is absent, forcing the effect to be 0 in the model, then the dummy variables of the interaction are extended to compensate. For example:

```
> model.matrix(~ wool+wool:tension, warpbreaks)
> model.matrix(~ tension+wool:tension, warpbreaks)
> model.matrix(~ wool:tension, warpbreaks)
```

The coding scheme for each factor is defined by a contrasts matrix of numerical values that are used to code the factor's dummy variables. The contrasts matrix for a k-level factor is a k × k−1 matrix with a row for each level of the factor and k−1 column vectors, each a pairwise contrast.

By default all factors have the same contrasts. The default scheme for unordered factors in R is called "treatment" contrasts.[22] Function contr.treatment generates a contrasts matrix for each factor given the number of levels. For example:

```
> contr.treatment(2)  # Contrast matrix for a 2-level factor (such as wool)
> contr.treatment(3)  # Contrast matrix for a 3-level factor (such as tension)
```

The first matrix provides two values for the dummy variable of the wool grouping factor, respectively coding levels A and B. The second provides three values for the two dummy variables of the tension grouping factor, respectively coding levels L, M, and H. The values for the two dummy variables of the wool:tension interaction

---

[20] Comparisons between all pairs of groups cannot be tested because only k−1 dummy variables are linearly independent. More than this leads to "aliasing", where some contrasts are linearly dependent upon others and a unique solution for all the parameters does not exist.

[21] Lower order terms are said to be "marginal" to an interaction that contains them, and should be present in the model. See: Nelder, J.A. (1977) "A reformulation of linear models". Journal of the Royal Statistical Society, Series A, 140, 48–77. Nelder, J.A. (1994) "The statistics of linear models: back to basics". Statistics and Computing 4, 221–234.

[22] Treatment contrasts are not proper "contrasts" since the coefficients do not sum to 0. Neither are they orthogonal. Nevertheless they are the default coding for dummy variables in R, mainly because they contrive comparisons that are relatively easy to interpret, even with unbalanced layouts.

are products of the codes of their respective components. For example showing the grouping factors alongside their coded dummy variables:

```
> dm = model.matrix(~ wool*tension, warpbreaks)
> data.frame(warpbreaks[-1], dm, check.names=F)
```

It is necessary to understand how contrasts represent pairwise differences and how the numerical values given to dummy variables are contrived so that the regression coefficients can be interpreted as differences between cell means. For example the codes of the dummy variables above form six regression equations, each describing the mean of the observations in a particular cell of the design. The first applies to observations in cell A|L, and is the intercept-only model: breaks~1. Therefore the intercept is the mean of the reference cell A|L, (the cell formed by the combination of first levels of the factors, the top-left in the table of cell means). The mean of cell B|L is described by model breaks~1+woolB. The intercept is the mean of A|L, and therefore the woolB coefficient is the mean difference between cells: B|L−A|L. Likewise coefficients woolB, tensionM, and tensionH all represent first-differences between cell means. The mean of cell B|M is described by model breaks~1+woolB+tensionM+woolB:tensionM. Here woolB and tensionM are first-differences between cell means with respect to the reference cell. Therefore the woolB:tensionM coefficient is the mean difference: B|M − [A|L + (B|L−A|L) + (A|M−A|L)], which reduces to: (B|M−B|L)− (A|M−A|L). Likewise interaction coefficients woolB:tensionM and woolB:tensionH are second-differences between cell means.

To summarise, when treatment contrasts are used the regression coefficients of the dummy variables represent differences between cell means as follows:

(Intercept)	A|L	44.6
woolB	B−A|L	28.2−44.6 = −16.3
tensionM	M−L|A	24.0−44.6 = −20.6
tensionH	H−L|A	24.6−44.6 = −20.0
woolB:tensionM	(M−L|B)−(M−L|A)	(28.8−28.2)−(24.0−44.6) = 21.1
woolB:tensionH	(H−L|B)−(H−L|A)	(18.8−28.2)−(24.6−44.6) = 10.6

Testing the Comparisons

The summary.lm tests regression coefficients, and summary.aov with its split argument tests partitions of the mean-squares. Both functions work in conjunction with the contrast coding system when the model includes factors. The summary.lm function tests the coefficient of each contrast-coded dummy variable. The summary.aov function has an argument named split that is used to specify partitions defined by the contrast coding. It is given a list in which each component is the index or name of a column of a factor's contrast matrix, (or a vector of indices or names to specify a partition as a sum of contrasts). For example[23]:

```
> fit = aov(breaks~wool*tension, warpbreaks)
> summary.lm(fit)
> summary.aov(fit, split=list(wool=1, tension=1:2, "wool:tension" = 1:2))
```

It is up to the user to ensure that the contrasts, and hence the partitions, are orthogonal or have a sensible interpretation.

Assigning Contrasts

The simplest way to test other comparisons without having to change the default contrast coding scheme is to change the reference level. This can be done using function relevel to change the first level of factors:

```
> warpbreaks$wool2 = relevel(warpbreaks$wool, "B")   # New factor
> fit2 = aov(breaks~ wool2*tension, warpbreaks)
> summary.lm(fit2)
```

By default all factors have the same contrasts. This can programmatically be overridden and customised globally for all factors or for individual factors. Individual factors can be assigned their own contrasts by attaching a contrasts attribute to the factor. The attribute's value may either be a contrasts matrix, or the name of a contrast generating function.[24] Factors with no contrasts attribute inherit their contrasts from a global option[25] named contrasts. This is the default condition for

---

[23] The p-values for corresponding 1-df tests are not the same because the default contrasts are not orthogonal and the partition sums-of-squares are not additive. Corresponding p-values are the same if orthogonal contrasts such as Helmert are used instead.

[24] Several convenience functions are provided to generate contrast matrices for commonly used contrasts. See help(contr.treatment). These include:

contr.treatment, for treatment contrasts, aka simple or dummy coding, (the default for unordered factors in R). The intercept is the mean of the reference cell, and other regression coefficients represent mean differences with respect to the reference cell.

contr.sum, for sum contrasts, aka deviation or effects coding, (the default in SPSS). The intercept is the grand mean, and other regression coefficients represent deviations from the grand mean.

contr.SAS, for contrasts like the default in SAS. Essentially like treatment contrasts but using the last level of factors to define the reference cell.

contr.helmert, for Helmert contrasts, aka contrast coding, (the default in S-Plus). Helmert contrasts in R are defined differently from Helmert contrasts in SAS or SPSS. There each level of the factor is compared with the mean of the succeeding levels. The R Helmert contrasts are more like "reverse" Helmert contrasts where each level of the factor is compared with the mean of the preceding levels.

contr.poly, for polynomial contrasts (for example for trend analysis, the default for ordered factors in R). See also contr.sdif in the MASS library.

[25] See help(options) and options("contrasts").

all factors, with the global contrasts option set to a vector of two function names: contr.treatment and contr.poly. The contr.treatment function is used with unordered factors, and the contr.poly function is used with ordered factors.

Contrasts can be assigned to factors in three ways:

1. Set the global contrasts option that will be inherited by all factors that do not have a contrasts attribute:

```
> options(contrasts=c("contr.sum","contr.poly"))        # Set global contrasts
> options(contrasts=c("contr.treatment","contr.poly"))  # Restore the defaults
```

2. Attach a contrasts attribute to an individual factor and assign either a contrasts matrix or the name of a contrast generating function using functions[26]: contrasts or C. The attached contrasts will override the global defaults each time this factor is used.

```
> contrasts(warpbreaks$wool)                            # Query contrasts
> contrasts(warpbreaks$wool) = "contr.helmert"          # Attach contrasts
> contrasts(warpbreaks$wool) = NULL                     # Detach contrasts
```

3. Assign contrasts temporarily to individual factors using the contrasts argument to functions lm or aov. For example assign polynomial contrasts to the tension factor during a call to lm, and test the linear and quadratic trend in the number of breaks as the tension changes through its three levels:

```
> fit.poly = lm(breaks ~ tension, warpbreaks,
                contrasts=list(tension="contr.poly"))
> summary.lm(fit.poly)
```

Assigning a Contrasts Matrix

A custom contrasts matrix is necessary when the required comparisons are not available from the provided contrast generating functions. For example testing simple main effects using interaction contrasts. Define a custom contrasts matrix to set up comparisons between the two types of wool at each of the three levels of tension. The matrix must have a row for each level in the interaction. Each column is a contrast.

```
>   #            "A:L"   "A:M"   "A:H"   "B:L"   "B:M"   "B:H"
>   K = cbind(  c(1,     0,      0,     -1,      0,      0),   # A − B|L
+               c(0,     1,      0,      0,     -1,      0),   # A − B|M
+               c(0,     0,      1,      0,      0,     -1))   # A − B|H
```

---

[26] If you provide less than k−1 contrasts for a k-level factor these functions will add orthogonal "filler" contrasts to make up a "complete comparison". See also: make.contrasts in package gmodels, and also function estimable in package gmodels and function glht in package multcomp.

The coefficients of each contrast should sum to 0. The contrasts, (including a column of 1's for the intercept), are mutually orthogonal if the cross-product matrix is diagonal.[27]

```
> colSums(K)                  # Contrast coefficients sum to zero
> crossprod(cbind(1, K))      # Orthogonal
```

Derive a new factor for the interaction and assign the contrasts matrix to that factor.[28] Fit the model and test the partitions defined by the contrasts:

```
> warpbreaks$wt = warpbreaks$wool:warpbreaks$tension   # The interaction
> contrasts(warpbreaks$wt) = K   # Attach the contrasts matrix to the factor
> fit = aov(breaks ~ wt, warpbreaks)
> summary.aov(fit, split=list(wt=list("wool|L"=1, "wool|M"=2, "wool|H"=3)))
> summary.aov(fit, split=list(wt=list("wool|L"=1, "wool|MH"=2:3)))   # Sum M and H
```

The interaction contrasts are equivalent to tests of simple main effects in which each F ratio is formed using the individual effect's between-groups variance in the numerator but the overall within-groups variance in the denominator.[29] For example:

```
> # Between-groups variance: MS wool at each level of tension
> summary(aov(breaks ~ wool, subset(warpbreaks, tension=="L")))   # 1200.5 on 1 df
> summary(aov(breaks ~ wool, subset(warpbreaks, tension=="M")))   # 102.72 on 1 df
> summary(aov(breaks ~ wool, subset(warpbreaks, tension=="H")))   # 150.22 on 1 df
> # Overall within-groups variance: the MS residual
> summary(aov(breaks ~ wool*tension, warpbreaks))   # 119.7 on 48 df
> # F tests
> pf(1200.5/119.7, 1, 48, lower.tail=F)   # 'wool' at tension 'L'
> pf(102.72/119.7, 1, 48, lower.tail=F)   # 'wool' at tension 'M'
> pf(150.22/119.7, 1, 48, lower.tail=F)   # 'wool' at tension 'H'
```

---

[27] Two contrasts are orthogonal if their sum-of-products (the inner product) is 0. The matrix cross-product contains the sum-of-products of all pairs of column vectors. The off-diagonal elements are the sum-of-products of pairs of different contrasts.

[28] It is not possible to assign contrasts directly to an interaction because contrasts for interactions are derived internally from the products of the component dummy variables. So it is necessary to create a new factor to represent the interaction and assign the contrasts to that factor. Assign the contrasts using the contrasts function in order to obtain an orthogonal "complete" comparison. Here there are three contrasts of interest, but the contrasts function automatically adds a further two orthogonal "filler" contrasts.

[29] This approach is appropriate when the group variances are reasonably similar. It is used here for illustration although the variances are not very similar.

5.4 Learning R

The best way to learn R is to use it. It is far better to use it than to read about it. The aim of this tiny handbook is to give you a roadmap with signposts to further information and documentation.

Begin with a simple job and a small data set. You might want to replicate some analysis previously done using a different program. Read the data into R, and use functions like `dim`, `names`, and `summary` to check your data frame. Calculate some summary statistics and plot some graphs. Save your script of commands in a text editor. Add comments to your script to remind you what it is doing.

Index